"The value of this book lies in the clear, concise description of steps to implementing TQM. No smoke, no mirrors, no fog; just the straight-forward facts and methods that can, and do, work."

Michael D. Jones, P.E.
Director, Arkansas Center for Quality
and Productivity

"Joe's expertise shines through in *Implementing TQM: Competing in the Nineties Through Total Quality Management*."

K. D. Lam
Vice-President of Corporate Improve-
ment
Imperial Holly Corporation

"Mr. Jablonski's book is an absolute must for those involved in the implementation of Total Quality Management in any organization. His book incorporates the concepts espoused by the TQM experts and provides an excellent methodology that directs one on a logical path to success. Read it!"

CDR Jon Lund, USN
TQM Coordinator
Field Command,
Defense Nuclear Agency

"Use of the logical and well-organized approach that Joe advocates greatly enhanced our organization's implementation program. Of the many books on TQM I have come across, I particularly like his inclusion of public-sector application of TQM principles and implementation strategy."

Russell K. Livingston
New Mexico District Chief
U. S. Geological Survey, Water Resources
Division

"In a world of fast-paced change, Joe has succeeded in creating a workable "how to" text on Total Quality Management. The exhibits and highlighting make it easy for the reader to get to the meat of the subject area quickly, but completely. Definitely a beneficial treatise for all who read it."

G. Lee Trussell
Partner
The Johnson-Trussell Company

"Joe's book serves our organization as a primer on surviving hyper-growth and serving our customers better. We've actually come to enjoy the knowledge of change in our processes."

Caroline Roberts
President, Computer One, Inc.

"Joe has effectively woven the need for participation in change into the fiber of his approach to TQM implementation. His prescription for success requires more than passive acceptance of change; it demands the active pursuit of fresh perspectives. Joe leads us through the process convincingly, offering a flexible, pragmatic, and realistic approach for initiating and managing TQM."

Rodney L. Stewart, CAPT., USN (Ret.)
Speaker and Seminar Leader
Rod Stewart and Associates

Implementing TQM:

Competing in the Nineties Through Total Quality Management

Revised Second Edition

by Joseph R. Jablonski

Foreword by Paul Hartman

Published by
Technical Management Consortium, Inc.
Albuquerque, New Mexico, USA

Published by:
> Technical Management Consortium, Inc.
> P.O. Box 13591
> Albuquerque, New Mexico 87192-3591
> USA

Library of Congress Catalog Card Number: 92-64219

ISBN 1-878821-09-1

Special appreciation to

Calline Cone, administrative assistance
Donna Fastle, editorial assistance
Paul Jones, desktop publishing
Mario and Jacque Ruiz, graphics services
Amory A. Miller, Jr., technical review

First Printing, April 1994
9 8 7 6 5 4 3 2 1

Printed in Michigan, U. S. A.

Dedication

To my sons Joey Jr. and Michael, who share my optimism for a brighter future.

I love you both

Contents

Foreword

Ford Motor Company, 1974: more than 80% of the automobiles leaving the assembly line go immediately to a rework facility—a factory within a factory. Ford Motor Company, 1978: an ultramodern Ford steel mill sells steel to small European countries, while Ford itself buys steel from Japan in order to get the quality necessary to build cars. Ford Motor Company, 1980: the steel mill closes, turns out the lights and locks the door. Soon many more Ford Motor Company plants, as well as those of other auto companies, will follow. Meanwhile, the desks of people trying to administer the myriad of functions of producing automobiles are piled high with paper—mostly multicopy forms with unclear, and sometimes unknown, destinations and functions.

During those years, I began questioning the way we were doing business at Ford Motor. In the mid 1970s, it became clear to me that the American automobile industry was not the only business unable to compete internationally. Information on methods the Japanese, our offshore competitors (as they are euphemistically referred to in the auto industry), were using did not seem to be available from the many top-management people I queried at Ford Motor and other businesses.

Researching this mystery, I eventually came upon my first clue: the Japanese designed quality into their vehicles. But what did that mean? We wouldn't know for many years. Our experience, knowledge, expertise, and arrogance would impede our learning. Indeed, it would be many years before we would even recognize the difference between attempting to achieve a deliverable product or service through inspection, and designing quality into a product or service.

But some people, including Joe Jablonski and I, continued searching and digging. The early 1980s brought the "Quality Circle" panacea—the concept of "let those doing the jobs tell us how we can improve." Interdepartmental teams studied procedures and made recommendations on quality improvement. However, the scope of these teams was limited, due to their inability to operate outside their immediate areas. And, as it turned out, the decision makers in this country—those who decided to get on the bandwagon with the other Quality Circle companies—were not interested. They had done their job in permitting the Quality Circles to exist. Quality Circles were like ships without rudders; those who had the influence to make them successful were not at the helm, so the circles drifted aimlessly upon the corporate seas.

In the mid 1980s, we learned that the Japanese were using Statistical Process Control (SPC) to identify problem areas. Soon control charts started appearing in abundance. Reports of factory walls being papered with control charts were common. But we didn't know how to use these charts, nor did we recognize that SPC involves a wide array of tools, beyond mere statistical information. Frequently, control charts served to monitor employees, rather than to help them understand processes.

Finally, in the late 1980s, all the tools, concepts, and philosophies of managing for quality merged under the name of Total Quality Management, or TQM. We began to understand that no single aspect of TQM could work by itself; TQM was a comprehensive management methodology consisting of many facets that had to be applied in a continually changing combination.

Leaders of American business and industry soon learned that in order to orchestrate TQM, a change in organizational culture had to be effected. Managers had to stop trying to manage *people* and learn how to manage *efforts*, to stop being bosses and start being leaders. Employees had to understand that they were no longer expected to "just do the job and don't ask questions"; instead, they were now expected to contribute to improving quality. But how does a corporation change the fundamental facets of its organizational culture?

The way people think about their organization reflects the organizational culture, and thoughts affect actions. Actions, in turn, provide the experience base by which an organizational culture is established. So, to effect cultural changes, management must modify the way people think, which, in turn, influences their actions. This can be a long and arduous endeavor, with no method for empirically measuring progress.

On the other hand, management could change its organizational culture by changing the way people do things, such as forming cooperative teams, rather than competitive departments. But operational procedures must be led by top management. Jamie Houghton, CEO of Corning Glass, a leader in TQM in this country, says that everybody else in the company is watching him. If he blinks, TQM will flounder at Corning Glass. Top management influences organizational culture by its actions; it also establishes a reward system to which people respond. Therefore, TQM can only be implemented by top management.

Many methodologies for implementing TQM exist, but to my knowledge, we have had no detailed how-to guide showing specifically what needs to be done to accomplish the goal. This book fills that void. It guides top managers, showing what they need to know and do to implement Total Quality Management.

Joe has personally seen the failings of business and industry, in both the public and private sectors, resulting from an overall inattention to quality. Through a discussion of "un-quality" and an explanation of the Malcolm Baldridge National Quality Award, you will gain an appreciation for the many facets of TQM.

Joe illustrates a phase-by-phase implementation process and describes what all top managers need to know about TQM. Though he sometimes takes a humorous approach to the discussion, his attention to detail serves the serious student well. From his prescription for top-management activities, through the recognition and rewards that will befall Process Action Teams (PATs), to strategies for involving suppliers in the same quality approaches, Joe paves the road to TQM success and a more efficient, more competitive organization..

Joe's Five-Phase Approach™ is unique. Step-by-step implementation methodologies become cumbersome when people in an organization don't respond in a lockstep fashion. The method outlined in this book accounts for overlapping phases, thereby allowing implementation strategies at various organizational levels to be pursued simultaneously.

The effective use of top management's time and resources is a critical thread running throughout the book. You will learn exactly what training executives need and where to get it.

Joe encourages the use of outside consultants, though he knows that consulting services can be expensive. So he teaches you when to hire outside consultants, how to find them, when to let them go, and how to get the most for your consultant dollar.

My own surveys and research indicate that quality has finally been dragged, albeit kicking and screaming, out of the "quality department" in most organizations. We are realizing that quality must be everybody's responsibility. Joe describes how to permeate quality throughout an organization. His guidelines for bringing PATs on line and having them interact with the Corporate Council assure a TQM strategy that makes quality everybody's business. Realizing that mass training overlooks many people until circumstances involve them in the TQM effort, Joe wisely shows how you can provide training as needed. This maximizes your training dollar, allowing people to use their new knowledge immediately, while it's still fresh in their minds.

You will learn about the cost of TQM as well. Much like any other investment in your business, you can expect some period of time to elapse before realizing a return. Though the initial investment may seem formidable, the return is--in most cases--far greater than on any other investment you will make in your company.

And so it is with this book, the Total Quality Management implementation guideline. Only you can determine its value to your organization. Every TQM application becomes as unique as a fingerprint. That's what makes this book a tremendous asset as an implementation guide. This flexible, malleable approach demonstrates techniques that apply to any organization where top executives are serious about implementing Total Quality Management.

Paul Hartman
Belfort Engineering &
Environmental Services, Inc.
Albuquerque, New Mexico

Preface

The goal of this book is to impart to you, the reader, a realistic, achievable process for implementing TQM in any organization. This methodical system, called the Five-Phase Approach ™, revolves around people—from the Chief Executive Officer (CEO)/President to the individual providing face-to-face contact with the customer. Through a series of examples and case studies, you'll learn what top-management commitment entails and how to propagate that support and enthusiasm throughout an organization.

Training, an essential element in any TQM program, is discussed throughout the book. By following this straight-forward, step-by-step approach, you'll discover the interrelationship of all of the steps required for establishing and sustaining a Total Quality Management process in your organization. Whether you're new to the study of quality or an old pro, I hope you'll find this book an enlightening, entertaining and invaluable resource.

Acknowledgements

I'd like to thank the following people who have helped in a myriad of ways in the development, preparation, and review of this book.

Content Interviews

Robert B. Baker
Carolyn Burstein
Mary Jo Coulehan
Larry Cox
Jack Denslow
Roland De Rose
Ronald R. Dressler
Larry Ecton
Burton M. Gifford
Bonnie L. Glass
Dr. Steven C. Graves
Robert W. Holkup
Kevin J. Hull
Rochelle M. Igrisan
Raymond E. Lambert
Judith Jossa-Stephen
Dr. Fred R. McFadden
Dr. Michael McFaul

Barry W. Miller
J. Howard Mock
Dr. Joe Mullins
Darren Munoz
Terry O'Brien
Thomas J. O'Neill
Michael G. Pazak
Richard J. Power
Gregg K. Price
Carrie Roberts
Michael Robinson
Marcy Serratt
Rodney L. Stewart
Frank W. Stoup III
Dr. Stanley M. Tarka Jr.
Richard Walker
William M. Winbert
Dr. Jack D. Whitfield

Jenny Wong

Book Reviewers

Terry L. Cook
Patricia J. Jablonski

Business Advisement

Mo Shahinpoor, Ph.D., P.E.
Walter Yoder, PhD.

Thank you all.

PAUL HARTMAN

Paul Hartman began learning, teaching, and using Total Quality Management more than seventeen years ago while working for Ford Motor Company. The quality movement of the early 1980s at Ford utilized many of the TQM concepts Paul has been teaching.

In 1982 while at Rockwell International Corporation, Paul trained top management in TQM tools and techniques. More than 150 process improvement teams were trained and facilitated under his guidance. Corporate functions benefiting from Paul's efforts include procurement, foundry operations, maintenance, word processing, employee benefits, machining operations, payroll, and waste management.

Paul is the TQM Consulting Specialist for Belfort Industries. He provides TQM services, including training in all TQM tools, techniques, concepts, and philosophies to government agencies, as well as to the private sector. Paul also facilitates TQM activities and provides consulting services. Organizations served by Paul include, the United States Department of Energy, Rockwell International, General Electric, EG&G, Inc., national laboratories, and health care facilities.

JOSEPH R. JABLONSKI

Joseph Jablonski is a speaker, trainer, and consultant, specializing in the design and implementation of Total Quality Management (TQM) systems and the application of TQM concepts in competitively bidding for work.

Joe serves clients throughout the United States and Canada in both private and public-sector organizations ranging in size from 10 people to 30,000 people. His work has benefited a wide variety of industries, including health care, professional services, architecture and engineering, temporary services, construction, government, mining, distribution, research and development, and others.

An active educator, Joe has developed, taught and coordinated classes, seminars, national videoconferences, and workshops on TQM, Project Management, Supplier Quality Systems, Competition and other related topics. In addition to numerous technical reports and articles, he is the author of the audio cassette seminar, *Achieving Total Service Quality*, published by the Institute for International Research, New York, NY and the soon-to-be released books *Prosper Through Leadership*.

Joe is a member of the Institute of Industrial Engineers (IIE), the American Society for Training and Development (ASTD), and the National Speakers Association (NSA), and is listed in the 1989 edition of *Who's Who in U.S. Executives.* He earned his bachelors and masters degrees in engineering from the University of New Mexico and was recently admitted into the *First International Who's Who in Quality*.

Joe has two sons, Joey Jr. and Michael. They make their home in Albuquerque, New Mexico.

Chapter 1. Introduction

World Immersed in Change

Change is a constant throughout life, and how we adapt to change determines whether we grow and evolve as individuals, or whether we become stagnant and inflexible. The same premise applies on a national and international level. Today, more than ever before, the world is immersed in change. Consider the dramatic events we've witnessed in recent years.

For 45 years or so, we lived in a bipolar world, with communist forces on one side and democratic forces on the other. That balance of power literally dominated worldwide events until the collapse of the Soviet Union. The creation of the Commonwealth in 1991 represents a major turning point in the course of history for all nations—not just the former Soviet Union.

At one time, military strength determined the global powers. This no longer holds true; in the 1990s global power hinges upon economic prowess. Soon the U.S. will have to contend with the giant economic power of the European Community (EC). Despite their differences, leaders of 12 nations—Belgium, Britain, Denmark, France, Germany, Greece, Ireland, Italy, Luxembourg, the Netherlands, Portugal, and Spain—have agreed that a common political purpose will improve their position in world affairs. Such an alliance will undoubtedly have a tremendous affect on international relations, as the remaining nations begin to adjust to the shift in power. Already American companies wanting to continue to do business in Western Europe are having to accommodate the developing ISO 9000 series of standards.

We see similar evidence of change within the Asian economic community. Japan, Singapore, Korea, and Taiwan, significant entities on their own, could merge to form another economic giant. We may even see the emergence of a North and South American economic community, if Mexico joins the free trade zone of the U.S. and Canada. Though the development of economic blocs sharply contrasts the political trends, who can predict what the future might hold? The only thing we know for certain is that things will change.

One-half of all the technological advances we enjoy today have been developed since 1900. Many items we take for granted—from antibiotics and latex paint to lap-top computers and fax machines—are relatively new. This innovative technology has brought forth new concerns as well. For example, we see a widespread sensitivity and heightened awareness of environmental issues. Fifteen years ago, our nation confronted environmental problems like untreated waste polluting bodies of water and toxic fumes billowing from smoke stacks. We attacked these problems in the U.S. and realized some "easy wins." But soon the widespread, worldwide scope of our past actions began to surface. Though some of these problems have been addressed, the world now faces more difficult, intractable international environmental issues with no readily apparent solutions.

However, a glimmer of hope lies within our children, who've become acutely aware of the environment. Not long ago I was watching Saturday morning cartoons with my sons, Joey Jr. and Michael, and in one particular episode, the villain attempted to introduce ozone eaters into the atmosphere. The hero's task was to stop him from releasing the ozone eaters. Suddenly my seven-year-old son, Michael, looked up at me and said, "Dad, we've got to save the earth." (My how times have changed. When I was a kid growing up in New Jersey, Saturday morning cartoon villains always tied damsels to railroad tracks.)

I believe that left to its own devices, the earth will take care of itself; "saving the earth" is truly not the issue. Mankind must stop destroying it so that we can continue to inhabit the planet. Ultimately, the solution entails personal responsibility. We must all take a leadership role in protecting our environment and strive toward a common focus. Much like TQM, we need to take action individually and work as a team. We can't afford to wait for someone else to take the initiative.

We live in a fast-paced society. Just keeping up with current events can be a challenge. As the rate of change increases, individuals and organizations need a way to manage that change—to make sense of it and put it in perspective. Total Quality Management, a change process within itself, provides an avenue for coping with change and directing it toward a positive outcome for the future.

TQM as a Change Process

To successfully implement any change process, we must address the systems in our business and the basic behaviors of our people to facilitate this change. In America today, the interest in quality extends into every competitive business and industry. For example, GMARA Industrial Cleaning, a joint venture between General Motors and ARA Services, adheres to a quality program that brought remarkable results for their customers and workforce alike. GMARA personnel take pride in improving things behind the scenes in the industrial cleaning area, working as part of a team with their customers—most often, plant populations of 2,000 to 3,000 people.

New employees receive extensive classroom training through lectures, discussions, and reading materials. This formal education instills an attitude of professionalism. At GMARA, employees develop self-esteem early on, as they learn that dedicated managers and supervisors do the same line of work. They also receive individual attention from a team of industrial cleaning implementers, helping them devise an employee development plan. Training sessions follow periodically, to expand their knowledge of tools and requirements.

Jobs are designed so that performance is measurable. It's easy to measure square footage cleaned, but in establishing a benchmark, various attributes—such as the amount of dirt and the type of floor covering—must be considered and adjusted for. Then the general standard can be modified accordingly. This careful measurement helps employees realize that management fully understands all aspects of their work.

Beyond enjoying a clean work environment, GMARA customers have reaped unexpected benefits as well—such as a simplified waste disposal system. Under GMARA's management, companies that previously used 400-500 different products through an unmanaged cleaning force have learned to consolidate and eliminate 60 percent of them. This not only decreases the possibility of error in the products' use, but also simplifies waste disposal and reduces the amount of Environmental Protection Agency (EPA) reporting required—an expensive and time-consuming procedure. GMARA's commitment to service excellence is reflected in its climbing sales figures—over 30 percent a year. At this company, everyone learns not only to accept what they do, but to do it with enthusiasm.

Implementing TQM also changes the behavior of management significantly. Practices considered beneficial just a few years ago are now dated and outmoded. Joe Mullins, who has directed several AT&T laboratories, has witnessed a great deal of corporate change in the past few decades. One of the major trends he sees is industry's shift toward fewer managerial positions, with more teams and informal leaders. In the old autocratic or perhaps "paternalistic" management style, the leader took pride in understanding all the details and running the organization directly. Today, however, there are too many details for one individual to handle as the spans of control increase.

So organizations are flattening out—replacing managers with people who act more informally, as leaders, teachers, or advisors. TQM philosophy fits right into this process, because the people reporting to the manager require self-direction and self-motivation. Therefore, managers can become far more efficient by teaching and coaching their people toward more independent decision making.

It's a difficult transition, especially for managers and employees raised in the old school. But it can be accomplished. Not long ago, Ted Sahd, a friend of mine, told me about a technical division at Wright-Patterson Air Force Base run by a person with a Ph.D. in psychology. When asked how he could lead all those highly-specialized technical managers, the psychologist replied, "Because I don't have the technical knowledge, I don't threaten them and they know that I trust their word."

As the world becomes more complex and new information bombards us at every turn, this new management style is becoming the trend. Effective managers will spend less time overseeing the jobs being done and more time helping their staff learn how to solve problems independently. This does not mean that engineering managers need not have the same good grasp of engineering issues. The fact that only 20% of CEOs in U.S. manufacturing are engineers, as opposed to some 80% in Japan, may indicate something significant. However, micromanagement of engineering projects by management is not the wave of the future. Instead, team and participatory approaches have become the definite trend.

No doubt, change is imminent in our society. An organization positioned for change will succeed and in doing so, redefine the standards for its competitors. In contrast, those unwilling or unprepared for change will be left behind–victims of the change process.

As the World War II British Prime Minister of "blood, sweat, and tears" fame, Sir Winston Churchill, once said, "There is nothing wrong with change if it is in the right direction. To improve is to change, so to be perfect is to have changed often." To constantly strive for change and create a willingness on behalf of your people to participate in this change is to practice TQM.

The Need to Improve the Way We Do Business

The motives for pursuing quality differ from company to company. In an extremely competitive, price-conscious industry, an organization's need for TQM becomes readily apparent. For example, Summit Electric Supply Company, a distributor with 150 employees in six locations, serves the construction market, an industry known for tight profit margins. Summit's customers include anyone buying electrical products—primarily electrical contractors and industrial and commercial organizations. It costs customers money to have someone waiting in line at the counter for supplies, so Summit's staff works at a fast tempo.

To stay ahead of the competition, Summit sells quality as a value-added service, introducing revolutionary ideas into a very traditional business. By learning to anticipate customers' requirements, Summit has redefined electrical distribution sales and service within its market areas. The company pursues every reasonable method for gaining customer feedback, seriously asking customers to measure its performance against the competitors. How customers respond to these inquiries represents a behavioral change in and of itself. Before TQM, if you called a customer and asked how your product or service was performing for them, a common reaction might have been, "Gee, what is wrong? You wouldn't be asking unless there was a problem."

Summit wants to create a "revolution in customers' expectations," a term coined by their Quality Coordinator, Larry Ecton, by demonstrating that all supply houses are not alike. As a result of the quality-related innovations, the company has enjoyed more than 20 percent growth per year in a basically flat industry. In essence, the pie may be getting smaller, but Summit Electric Supply Company is gaining a larger percentage of that pie.

Some industries, however, are just discovering the need for TQM. For example, the prevailing philosophy in the concrete industry has been that of providing a commodity. After all—a yard of concrete is a yard of concrete. Aside from variations in price, manufacturers in this industry offer a very similar product. But the San Juan Concrete Company introduced a customer-service perspective into its business, differentiating it from other competitors.

San Juan Concrete Company produces sand and gravel, ready-mix concrete and hot-mix asphalt for commercial and residential contractors. When management decided to concentrate on improving customer service, TQM techniques helped educate the 90 employees in defining and delivering good service.

In this industry, customers usually select their suppliers based on price. But after the sale occurs, service factors come into play. Customers typically place an order and expect delivery within 30 minutes to an hour. In that brief amount of time, the company must manufacture the right amount and type of product (consisting of an average of eight or nine components), load it into a truck, and deliver it to the customer's job site—the epitome of a Just-In-Time (JIT) operation. In order to accommodate this extremely short turn-around time, every process must be evaluated and improved wherever possible.

Even established industry leaders strive for continuous process improvement, as in the case of Wal-Mart. This company began its climb to the top in 1945, when Sam Walton opened Walton's Ben Franklin in Newport, Arkansas. Today 1,747 Wal-Mart stores and 220 Sam's Clubs thrive in 43 states and in Puerto Rico. No matter how you look at it, that represents nearly 50 years of phenomenal growth and progress.

Until the end of the 1980s, Sears had led the industry for decades. In fact, I grew up wearing Sears jeans, because my mom could pay for them over a period of time, using her Sears revolving charge account. But in late 1990 and early 1991, Wal-Mart's sales surpassed both Sears and K-Mart and became the nation's largest retailer.

This company had never set the goal of becoming the "largest," only on becoming the "best." Because Sam Walton lived the philosophy of, "If we're standing still, we're going backwards," he encouraged new ideas. Even after his corporation had attained unprecedented success, "Mr. Sam" sought ways to improve operations in his stores. For instance, after hearing about other companies' activities in the quality arena he said, "That sounds like something that we really need to incorporate into our company (For our associates and our customers)." So it's important to realize that highly successful organizations pursue TQM too—especially if they want to remain on top.

Although companies implement TQM for a variety of reasons, the outcome is the same: an improved competitive position and a common vocabulary. American consumers have become intrigued by the subject of quality. Though they may not be able to articulate its precise meaning, they recognize—and appreciate—quality when they see it. Organizations that fail to speak the language and develop systems to ensure quality goods and services will not survive. The need for quality today is no longer a veiled threat; there is no veil.

Quality Pays

The U.S. General Accounting Office (GAO) conducted a review of the 20 highest-scoring applicants for the Malcolm Baldrige National Quality Award over a two-year period to evaluate the impact of TQM practices on their organizations. Although each company developed its system in a unique environment, in nearly all cases those using TQM techniques achieved better employee relations, greater customer satisfaction, higher productivity, improved profitability, and increased market share. Similar results have been seen in companies that have applied for the prestigious Deming Prize in Japan. The results, which represent four decades of experience, confirm a distinctive relationship between quality and profit.

Employee-related indicators proved an extremely important feature in implementing a successful TQM system. The GAO survey rated the factors pertaining to employee performance. Clearly, employee safety/health, employee satisfaction, and attendance serve as very positive indications that an organization is providing a valuable service to its employees through the quality process.

Within this same survey, customer satisfaction encompassed issues of overall satisfaction, customer complaints, and retention rates. A variety of industries have found that it takes one-fourth as much company resources to keep an existing customer than to attract a new one. So customer satisfaction and retention are important factors in any successful quality process.

In terms of financial performance, we see similar positive results. Market share increased for 9 of the 11 reporting companies, consistent increases in sales per employee, return on assets, etc. Undoubtedly, the employee and customer results above contributed in a significant way. Officials from the two companies experiencing a decrease attributed that decline to increased foreign competition.

Other studies of TQM's impact on corporate performance have resulted in similar conclusions. For example, The Conference Board, Inc., a New York business research group, surveyed senior executives at large U.S. corporations about their quality management practices. Of 149 firms responding, 111 had a quality management program in place, and 13 said they plan to institute TQM.

In order for such change to take place, the very foundation of an organization, the corporate culture, must be addressed. An organization's culture is defined as the set of values, beliefs, and behaviors that form its core identity. Quality companies agree that an open, responsive culture is the key to a firm's future competitiveness—or even survival. Open corporate cultures share the following characteristics: widespread information-sharing, fewer barriers among departments and workers, a spirit of innovation, and a high level of employee satisfaction. The systematic and behavioral aspects of any successful quality process are inseparable; each closely influences the other, as we will see when we move into the discussion of the implementation process.

The Origin of TQM

Most TQM training courses attribute the foundation of TQM to Dr. W. Edwards Deming's and Dr. Joseph Juran's efforts to revitalize Japan's crumbling economy after World War II, at the request of General MacArthur. Beaten militarily and economically, Japan's quality and manufacturing techniques ranked poorly in worldwide competition. However, the Japanese possessed an uncanny ability to copy. In fact, Japan had a town named Usa (pronounced oo-sa), and products manufactured in this area bore the label, "Made in USA," in an attempt to capitalize on the quality reputation the United States held at that time.

Japan's transformation from "copier" to "leader" began when Deming and Juran introduced the Statistical Quality Control (SQC) concept of management, a statistical theory originated by Sir Ronald Fisher over 70 years ago. During World War II Walter Shewhart, a Bell Laboratories physicist, used this theory to develop the zero-defects approach to producing telephones. Deming, who had worked with Shewhart, developed his own version of SQC, which he introduced to Japan. Japan's emergence as an economic powerhouse can be directly attributed to the application of these concepts.

However, to find the very earliest hints of TQM, we must look beyond the basic concepts of SQC and process variability. Careful research reveals that the fundamentals of TQM philosophy date back to the "Penney Idea" of 1913—the seven tenants on which J.C. Penney was built:

1. To serve the public, as nearly as we can, to its complete satisfaction.

2. To expect for the service we render a fair remuneration and not all the profit the traffic will bear.

3. To do all in our power to pack the customer's dollar full of value, quality, and satisfaction.

4. To continue to train ourselves and our associates so that the services we give will be more and more intelligently performed.

5. To improve constantly the human factor in our business.

6. To reward men and women in our organization through participation in what the business produces.

7. To test our every policy, method, and act in this way: "Does it square with what is just and right?"

By 1940 J.C. Penney had 1,586 stores and sales of $300 million. There were no employees or clerks in these stores. Instead, Mr. Penney referred to his staff members as "associates." He created this term in the early days, while seeking a means for expansion. To provide the needed capital for opening new J.C. Penney stores, he invited his managers to save up and become partners in the company.

The Penney Idea espouses customer satisfaction, fairness, quality, value, associate training, and rewards for performance. The phrase, "To test our every policy, method and act," represents what we refer to today as empowering our people to challenge the status quo and arming them with the tools of continuous process improvement to create positive change. The basic concept of TQM isn't new; those who have prospered in American business recognize how to tailor these simple concepts to their own industry. And contrary to popular belief, the "Total" in TQM was founded in the service sector in America—not in the manufacturing industry. So when thinking of America's quality greats, maybe we should add John C. Penney's name to the list.

It's easier to implement TQM when its basic philosophy aligns with your personal beliefs. Consider Wal-Mart, for example, with its emphasis on people. Associates wear the slogan, "Our People Make the Difference," right on their name badges. This focus on people began with the company founder, Sam Walton, who recognized that the strength in a company lies in its people. But this attitude existed long before the corporation. Sam Walton was always known a "people person." In fact, his college yearbook describes him as, "the person who knew the names of all the janitors." Further, his scholastic record reflects his determination to achieve excellence.

Throughout his life, "Mr. Sam" understood his priorities. For example, vendors who visit the home office are often surprised to see people sharing an office, with used furniture at that. Mr. Sam believed in putting the money where it counts—in the stores. For a man of great vision, he maintained simple tastes. In 1989 he finally traded in his beat-up pick-up truck for a new one. But he mentioned to several people that it just wasn't the same.

Today as you thumb through the yellow pages of a telephone book, you'll see advertisements for quality automobile parts, quality dry cleaning services, quality health care, and so forth. The real challenge today is not to *say* you are a quality organization, but to *demonstrate* quality in the goods and services you provide. IBM's CEO John Akers expressed it well: "I am sick and tired of visiting plants to hear nothing but great things about quality and cycle time—and then to visit customers who tell me of problems." We hear lots of talk about quality, but as long as customers are still complaining, we haven't reached our goal.

TQM in Private and Public Sectors

We see abundant examples of TQM operating in private industry. Many companies, such as Summit Electric Supply, are making innovative changes on behalf of American consumers. For example, Summit Electric Supply Company does not believe customers should expect to stand in line, so they've issued a guarantee. If it takes more than 30 seconds for a customer to receive assistance at the counter, that customer receives a $5.00 coin, redeemable at Summit's counter.

About ten percent of Summit's sales stem from systems contracts—a form of partnership between the supplier and the customer. Basically, customers agree to purchase all (or most) of their electrical products from Summit; in return, they get extraordinary service and guaranteed pricing levels. They also benefit from free consulting and training for planning future projects. Entering into a systems contract with Summit Electric Supply Company significantly increases cost savings, reduces prices, and assures a very high level of quality. Summit has built a strong reputation on having the right products at the right place at the right time.

Every detail—right down to providing legible paperwork—has been examined from the customers' perspective. As a result, customers find they can save time and money by depending upon Summit as their strategic supplier.

In government, TQM techniques are also being used as a means of curtailing waste. For example, at Kirtland Air Force Base (KAFB), the Air Force Stock Fund, which operates as a bank account, experienced a substantial deficit, even though the customers paid a surcharge for purchases of supplies and equipment. To curtail the deficit, the process owner, Chief of Supply, sought volunteers knowledgeable in the process to form a team and select a leader. The KAFB quality organization provided a team facilitator and an on-call statistician. The facilitator provided training in data collection, interviewing, and JIT concepts. In two-hour weekly meetings, the team reviewed customer requirements, purchase requests, initial item descriptions, processing and pricing procedures of vendors, and delivery lead times. Then the statisticians and analysts portrayed the data in a user-friendly format, so the Chief of Supply and the Quality Council could see the variation built into the process.

This measurement proved most intriguing. Customer interviews revealed that what the customer wanted, what the customer ordered, and what the customer actually received commonly got tangled within the process. After confirming the data, the team prepared recommendations into a briefing for the Quality Council. All team members contributed to the final report, using tools such as check sheets, flow charts, cause-and-effect diagrams, force-field analyses, histograms, and Pareto, run, and control charts.

The team approach to process improvement revealed the instability of the current process. Measuring and eliminating variation improves the process and enables an organization to benchmark to excellence and define the total cost of quality implementation. In government, as in private industry, leadership must help manage changes—from recognizing the need for improvement to initiating action.

The Defense Contract Management Area Operations (DCMAO) Phoenix, a part of the Defense Contract Management Command (DCMC), was created in June 1990 to improve and streamline contract management within the Department of Defense (DoD).

Consequently, individual service organizations performing contract and major program management were abolished in favor of a single DoD element reporting directly to the Secretary of Defense. This action fulfilled a major recommendation of the Defense Management Review (Packard Commission).

Inherent in the establishment of the DCMC was a commitment to change the way contract and program management within the DoD were performed. The major change centered around providing a more customer-focused approach, intended to increase performance in an environment of reduced budgets, increasing competition for defense business, and reducing the time required for buying new systems and maintaining stock levels.

This program provided a foundation for building an organizational vision, complete with guiding principles and employee expectations. These, along with the commander's expectations, were used to form three Quality Management Boards (QMB)–Customer Focus, Business Practices, and People–made up of both workers and management striving to increase customer satisfaction, improve processes, and address personnel needs.

Operationally, under the broad direction of the Business Practices QMB, program support teams were created to provide program managers with an integrated assessment of major program status at contractor facilities. These assessments focus on program cost, schedule, and quality issues, not just stand-alone functional assessments. The In-Plant Quality Evaluation (IQUE) program allows the DCMAO to make product acceptance decisions on behalf of its customers (other organizations within government) based upon objective evidence of contractor performance. Customer requirements are identified through contractor site visits and surveys.

Another change resulting from the internalizing of TQM as a "way of life" has been the formation of divisional and functional/multi-functional Process Action Teams throughout the organization. The concept of TQM has become accepted and embraced as a way of doing business in resolving and improving the processes in which everyone works. This has facilitated the working team concept in the organization and has brought a better understanding of issues such as empowerment, ownership and accountability.

How successful has DCMAO been? They are making inroads; two-and-a-half years ago 320 people were in DCMAO Phoenix; now there are 265. The workload has not decreased significantly; in fact they have assumed additional roles and missions. Customers are extremely happy with the new and better products they are receiving, as the organization meets or beats every traditional workload measure. DCMAO Phoenix personnel want to do a good job and the more they know about their customers, the more they can do for them. This could not have occurred without the upfront planning investment in Total Quality Management.

TQM as It Applies to Small Companies

It's easy to see how quality applies in a large company with lots of resources, but 84% of all American companies have less than 50 employees. The federal government defines a small business as one with fewer than 500 employees, or $30M in annual sales. And during a 1990 workshop on the subject of TQM in government contracting, a representative of Martin Marietta Corporation suggested a small company is one with less than one billion dollars in annual sales. I personally subscribe to the "less than 50 employees" definition, since so many companies fit into this category.

Yet small businesses are making great strides in quality-improvement initiatives. For example, Marlow Industries, with 160 people, was the third small company to receive the prestigious Malcolm Baldrige National Quality Award, of 104 small business applications from the inception of the award in 1988. Let's look at two excellent examples of how small companies apply quality to their day-to-day business practices.

First, consider the accomplishments of Mike Robinson, former General Manager of the Albuquerque Marriott Hotel, and present owner of the Ozarka Lodge in Eureka Springs, Arkansas, a 100-year-old seasonal resort with 45 rooms. Mike learned about TQM through his work at the Marriott. Impressed with the results, he adapted that quality program to suit a much smaller operation. In contrast to the Marriott's several hundred employees, the Ozarka employs two people (Mike and his wife, Janie) during the off-season, and up to eight full-time and three part-time workers during the peak season. A true small company by any measure.

After assessing his staff's training needs, Mike presented a half-day orientation session. In plain, simple language, he spoke about the new goals of improvement and commitment. He explained that the staff could expect pay increases based upon the contributions they made to the growth of the Lodge, rather than length of service.

Then he led the group through team-building exercises to strengthen cohesiveness. For technical skills training, the staff divided into groups; Janie discussed specific procedures with the front office people, while Mike worked with the housekeeping people, outlining the room standards.

Mike began the TQM initiative by evaluating the status quo and looking for areas needing improvement. He focused on little things, realizing that they add up to big improvements. For instance, he noticed that no employee feedback system existed, so he instituted the Idea Form. When employees observe a problem, they fill out a card, stating the nature of the problem and suggesting a solution. To add incentive, Mike added a reward. The employee who submits the most Idea Forms each month receives a $20.00 bonus. This simple system yielded significant improvements in just four months of operation.

Next, Mike introduced the idea of tracking housekeepers' productivity in terms of person-hours per room. Mike evaluates productivity every day and provides feedback to the employees, who chart their own productivity on the wall in the housekeeping area. Since pay raises are tied to productivity, the staff has a good incentive. As a result, total housekeeping hours have dropped from 1.5 person-hours per occupied room to 1 hour, with an eventual goal of 45 minutes.

TQM does look different in a small organization. Small-scale operations have fewer resources, but they also require fewer. At the Marriott, for example, a TQM rally could involve several thousand dollars and a great deal of preparation time. In contrast, a rally for the Ozarka Lodge during the off-season might consist of Mike and Janie going out to dinner. The reduced need for a large dollar investment ties directly into the inherent strengths of all small organizations. Top-management commitment and communication are two key ingredients in any TQM process. Mike and Janie know their staff is getting the message, because they work side-by-side every day.

Now let's look at an entirely different small business, Computer One™, a woman-owned Apple Computer, Inc. dealer in Albuquerque, New Mexico, with 21 associates. In addition to the $7.5 million they averaged in 1991 equipment sales, they perform a variety of services—such as technical and logistics support by telephone, prompt dispatch, and 24-hour warranty service. They also provide a free training package, covering all products sold through their JIT system.

Computer One wants customers to realize the advantage of doing business with one dealer, so the company builds very specifically on the customers' needs. For instance, after a year's history of delivering on-time service at a level of 95 percent or above to Sandia National Laboratories, they have begun to concentrate on getting more of the items only occasionally needed by Sandia to further improve service. In many ways, Computer One serves as an extension of their customers' organization. Since communication occurs over the telephone and through a paperless system, they can easily adapt to using the customers' paperwork whenever a product leaves or returns to Computer One.

TQM applies particularly well to a small business in the realm of process improvement, especially in a company experiencing rapid growth. Small businesses can implement change and evaluate the results much faster than large organizations. At weekly planning meetings, every associate can contribute feedback and offer ways to improve.

And customer feedback can come quite quickly, too. Not long ago, Chris, a Computer One technician, provided training in the field for five Sandians. As soon as he left the site, the supervisor picked up the phone and called Caroline Roberts, President of Computer One, to let her know that Chris had done an outstanding job in training the entire section on using their new Macintosh. Normally, negative feedback travels much faster than positive comments. When a customer goes out of his or her way to compliment an associate's performance, you know you're doing something right.

The trend of quality in American industry is moving toward the smaller companies. As many industry giants implement quality processes, they reach a natural point where they must turn to their providers of goods and services for help in achieving the next level of excellence. And in many cases, these suppliers are very small companies with very big futures.

Problem Company: Tell-Tale Signs

We've all heard that "ignorance is bliss." This is true, at least in the short term. I once heard the following story about a perception of quality. "On the first of every month, quality was king. Management spoke of quality and encouraged improvement of quality. Defective products and services were nipped in the bud and corrected prior to ever making it into the hands of the customer. But, as the first of the month passed and the middle of the month approached, quality took on a new meaning. As the end of the month came closer, the motto became, 'ship it and we'll fix it in the field,' or 'we'll accept it as a return later. But for now, we can book the shipment and look good on paper.'"

The bliss of ignorance is reflected in the short-sighted type of management just described. Managers often do not recognize the problems with the way they conduct business, or they would surely change their ways. For that reason, I elected to include this section, so that management might better understand the "tell-tale signs of un-quality."

This understanding of un-quality was first brought to my attention by a young woman who noticed two key points that had eluded me in my own experience on this important subject. First, she recognized certain things one could notice, or better yet look for, that would suggest the need for improvement. Second, and most important, she observed a cyclic behavior to un-quality; it feeds on itself. In sharp contrast to TQM, where you are continually moving to improve the way you do business, un-quality continually degrades quality, productivity, and most importantly, employee morale.

The signs of un-quality are displayed in Exhibit 1-1. A department, division, or entire organization may enter this cycle at any point. Let us say, the quality of goods and services in a company decreases. The reason at this point is unimportant. We notice the time necessary to accomplish this process increases. This may be the result of conflict between personnel, unclear procedures, or any number of reasons. Usually as a reflex response, management increases the number of inspections. This makes sense under the traditional way of doing business. Employees can't be trusted to "do it right the first time"; therefore, we will "inspect quality in." As a result, morale suffers and workers—often the better employees—begin to leave.

EXHIBIT 1-1
Signs of Un-Quality

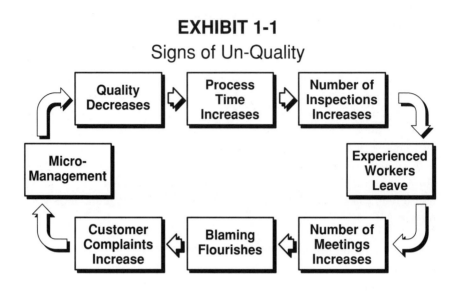

The number of management meetings increases to discuss this growing problem; finger-pointing flourishes; and the phone rings constantly with customer complaints. Management concludes these problems are obviously the fault of the workers. Therefore, they respond by managing the work force more, not better (also known as micro-management). We have now come full circle, and because of the accumulation of bad management decisions, we witness further quality deterioration. The cycle goes on and on.

The sequence of events may differ from company to company, but the outcome remains the same. Early on, the effects of reduced quality are hidden from management by shipping poor quality goods or providing inadequate services. The books look good because quotas are made, but the hidden problems resurface elsewhere later, usually for an increased cost. Your best employees leave, and it is difficult to hire the better prospects off the street because you have a bad reputation. Field returns rise, and you find yourself fixing problems at about 100 times the amount it would have cost to correct them in the plant or prevent in the first place.

Last, and most important, morale deteriorates and the traditional barriers between management and labor are further reinforced, because the workforce was blamed before the cause of the problem was even understood.

Poor credibility between management and labor intensifies, because quality standards were conveyed as a variable. Products and services of unacceptable quality on the first of the month were shipped on the 30th regardless. To the employees, there were no standards to follow.

I could go on describing how the cycle continues, eventually resulting in lost sales and lost jobs, but that is not the point. The important point is that management can recognize tell-tale signs and identify opportunities for improvement. If you can relate to any of these comments, I will have been half-successful by merely getting you thinking. If you go one step further and say you are going to do something about your company's problems and use TQM as your vehicle to success, we will both succeed.

Chapter 2. TQM: The Basics

Total Quality Management Defined

Attempts to define TQM have lead to many wandering conversations, meandering trails of misunderstanding and voluminous descriptions. To cut through much of this verbiage and confusion, I would like to offer my own definition of this important term.

TQM is:

> *A cooperative form of doing business that relies on the talents and capabilities of both labor and management to continually improve quality and productivity using teams.*

Joseph R. Jablonski

Embodied in this definition are the three ingredients necessary for TQM to flourish in any company: (1) participative management; (2) continuous process improvement; and (3) the use of teams.

Participative management comes about by practicing TQM. Arming your people with the skills and support to better understand how they do business, identifying opportunities for improvement, and making change happen will allow participative management to flourish. Recognizing the capabilities and contributions employees can make to improve business will begin to chip away at the traditional barriers that separate management and labor. This does not happen overnight and will only occur if management listens, and the workforce feels intimately involved with the ownership of the process.

For example, before TQM, supervisors receiving new company guidance on material management would probably go into their office, close the door and begin writing the new procedures to implement this guidance. After TQM, however, supervisors would invite the clerical, administrative, and support personnel who will eventually implement the new method to read the new company guidance, interpret it, and develop the procedures.

Participative management, unlike a light switch, cannot simply be turned on. It is an evolutionary process of trust and feedback which develops over time. Those first few steps toward participative management are slow; momentum builds gradually. Traditional barriers between management and labor must be breached by that entity willing to take the plunge and offer a show of faith. That is management's responsibility.

Continuous process improvement (CPI) means accepting small, incremental gains as a step in the right direction toward Total Quality. It recognizes that substantial gains can be achieved by the accumulation of many seemingly minor improvements whose synergies yield tremendous gains over the long run. Continuous process improvement reinforces a basic tenant of TQM—long-term focus. Corporate leaders must be willing to make an investment in Total Quality *today*, recognizing that big gains may lie in their future. In fact, the implementation approach described later recommends employees practice their new-found skills on small, achievable victories to improve processes. This approach not only allows employees to develop confidence in the TQM process, but also provides management with many opportunities to show support and encouragement.

Let me offer one example of continuous process improvement. When I first went to work for the government, it took about six weeks to process a travel claim. After returning from a trip, I would complete a travel claim and submit it for payment. Six weeks later I would have a check in hand. Through a series of CPIs this six-week cycle time became two weeks–a substantial improvement. I told that story to a group in Rosslyn, Virginia in the summer of 1991, and a woman from

Headquarters Defense Nuclear Agency in Alexandria said that if you submit a travel claim to her branch by 10:30 AM, your check would be ready for pick-up by 4:00 PM. Imagine my surprise!

During a subsequent presentation to a group of government personnel, I told the story about the one-day turn around as the benchmark, the one to beat. A man in the audience said that his finance center processes travel claims and prepares the checks within 20 minutes–the administrative equivalent of Just-In-Time. The check is prepared while you wait. Even good processes can be improved.

Finally, TQM involves teams. Each team includes a cross-section of members who represent some part of the process under study: the individuals who work within the process; the suppliers of services and materials brought into the process; and its beneficiaries, the customers. We groom our people to recognize opportunities for improvement within our corporation, understand our business practices, apply a structured approach to problem solving, and offer management recommendations on where to apply scarce resources first, so as to realize the greatest gains. This approach empowers the people directly involved in the day-to-day operations of the corporation to improve their work environment. The employees are aligned with the corporation's goals for improvement. This personal commitment is achieved in exchange for individual and team rewards, recognition, and job security.

TQM employs many varieties of teams. Most often people think of the cross-functional type of team which has representation throughout the various department or groups within the organization. But as we'll see in Chapter 8, this is just one type of team.

The Six Principles of TQM

At the conclusion of Chapter 1, I described the tell-tale signs of un-quality. Let us now focus our attention on those positive characteristics that will allow you to implement TQM in your company successfully. I call these attributes the principles of Total Quality Management.

EXHIBIT 2-1

Principles of TQM

1. **Customer Focus**

2. **A Focus on Process as Well as the Results**

3. **Prevention versus Inspection**

4. **Mobilize Expertise of Workforce**

5. **Fact-Based Decision Making**

6. **Feedback**

(1) A Customer Focus - We all recognize that our time on the job is spent performing tasks that will somehow support a sale. Corporations are in business to provide goods and services in exchange for revenue. Although this concept is neither new nor surprising to us, we must regularly reinforce it at all levels within our organization. In moving toward TQM, we acknowledge the existence of many customers we may have overlooked in the past. This includes the customer outside an organization, who places orders with us. I refer to this customer as the big "C." In addition, there is a little "c," the customers within our company with whom we work on a daily basis. Little "c's" include graphics departments providing visual aid support, payroll processing bi-weekly employee checks, finance generating advances for corporate travelers, etc. We relate well to the big "C," but our support and enthusiasm oftentimes wane when we support the little "c's." This frequently results from our indirect compensation for these services. Because we do not exchange funds for these internal services, it is difficult to draw a connection between the services the little "c" provides and the revenue it receives. As we implement TQM, we shift to a heightened awareness of all our customers, both the big "C" and the little "c."

One of the best examples I've heard of the concept of big "C's" and little "c's" came from Rochelle Igrisan, Associate Administrator of Perinatal Nursing at Sinai Hospital in Detroit. When this 615-bed major medical facility started a TQM initiative, the staff had trouble defining the "customer."

Traditionally, the patients are the hospital's customer, since they receive the services. But the Sinai staff realized that physicians are also big "C's," because they usually select the hospital for the patient.

Serving the patient well requires teamwork and cooperation among many departments. The nursing staff can't care for patients properly unless the pharmacy provides the medication, the lab performs the tests, and so forth. In essence, each department is a little "c" to every other department in the hospital. Recognizing this interdependence, the Sinai staff formed committees with members of various departments to study areas needing improvement.

When these committees examined the process of patient care–rather than the process of an individual department–they gained a new perspective. For example, the discharge staff pointed out that sometimes a patient's release was delayed by having to wait for lab test results. So the lab personnel modified their routine and scheduled the tests for early morning, rather than late afternoon. This change in the work flow of one department's internal process improved the over-all process of patient care.

In such a large organization, employees are usually surprised to be asked to contribute their knowledge and ideas. But the seeds for process improvement lie within every individual involved in the effort. Every little "c" understands the needs and expectations of the big "C's" from a different point of view. Working together, the little "c's" can find new ways to solve problems and improve processes–both for the big "C's" and the little "c's" alike.

One company with a long history of commitment to the customer is Hershey Foods Corporation, the leading chocolate and confectionery manufacturer in North America. This Fortune 500 company employs 13,000 people on several continents. In the late 1980s, Hershey had been experimenting with the production of a heat-resistant chocolate bar, examining scientific literature and evaluating new technologies. But Saddam Hussein's invasion of Kuwait in August 1990 shifted the course of events for Hershey. Suddenly, the military was actively seeking a heat-resistant chocolate bar, made with real milk chocolate, that could withstand the temperatures of the Persian Gulf.

Of all the things to do in preparing for war, why focus on a chocolate bar? The military wanted to give our soldiers a familiar taste from home. Traditionally, chocolate has served as a morale booster, a pleasurable food that leaves people with psychological and sensual satisfaction. Further, the U.S. Military Forces fielded in the Persian Gulf represented one of the youngest armies in the nation's history. Given this new customer demand, Hershey shifted into high gear. Producing a good heat-resistant chocolate bar was no longer an academic exercise–it was an emergency!

Hershey's R&D people reiterated the fact that an Army marches on its stomach. They wanted to provide something special for our troops, something that hadn't been sealed in a can or a pouch for a decade or so. With new-found commitment, various groups within the corporation formed teams, working long hours, weekends, and holidays. Despite the haste, Hershey never sacrificed quality. They adhered to their Product Excellence Program, maintaining the same standards for ingredients and processes involved in every Hershey's product. The packaging suppliers put forth a superb effort, too. Normal six-month delivery times dropped to eight weeks. No one worried about profit margins; everyone wanted to support the soldiers. And on December 4, 1991, the first shipment of Hershey's new one-ounce Desert Bars® headed toward Saudi Arabia. Our troops enjoyed chocolate for Christmas.

Hershey Foods Corporation has a rich history in working with the military. In fact, the first heat-resistant chocolate bar ever sold to the military, the Field Ration D bar, was produced by Hershey prior to World War II. And roughly 30 years later, Hershey refined and improved this product for our troops in Vietnam. Hershey will celebrate its 100-year anniversary in 1994, and a large measure of this corporation's success can be attributed to the founder, Milton S. Hershey, who wanted to provide a quality chocolate to the masses at an affordable price.

In 1991 these "masses" once again included the U.S. troops on foreign soil, young men and women longing for a familiar flavor. The company that bears the name of Milton S. Hershey once again met America's needs in the Persian Gulf with a quality chocolate product--The Desert Bar.®

(2) A Focus on the Process as Well as the Results - We are the customer for goods and services both from within and outside our company. When we receive a product that does not meet or exceed our expectations, we traditionally go to a competitor or complain, if we think it might get results. Under TQM, we use these deficient results, or un-met expectations, as symptoms—indicators that something is amiss with the process that pro-duced them. Later in the second phase of this implementation methodology

(Chapter 7), we will see how these symptoms result in action to correct the deficiencies and continually move to improve the quality of goods and services, using a structured approach to problem solving.

(3) Prevention versus Inspection - Having placed attention on the process as well as the results in Principle #2, the application of Principle #3, Prevention versus Inspection, becomes readily achievable. Before TQM, managers believed they could inspect quality in. When something went wrong in the production of goods and services, as a knee-jerk reaction they provided more inspectors. Not so with TQM. Here we apply a structured approach to problem solving and make the necessary investment to understand the process and sources of process variation. We then provide process controls to ensure every product and service meets an acceptable, predictable quality. TQM Principle #3 directs attention toward the prevention of defective products and services, rather than the discovery of defects and deficiencies after resources have been spent.

(4) Mobilizing Expertise of the Workforce - A traditional management atmosphere assumes the workforce consists of mindless individuals wanting nothing more than a pay check. TQM changes this manner of thinking profoundly. First, we recognize that we can compensate individuals for their efforts in many ways; financial compensation is only one method. Studies have shown that individuals hire on and stay with a corporation for various reasons. The salary or wage is not the only reason, nor is it first and foremost. People like to feel appreciated, and TQM creates new, innovative ways to recognize individuals for their efforts. Second, your workforce represents a tremendous wealth of knowledge and opportunity to improve the way you do business, increase profits, and reduce costs. A movement toward TQM mobilizes the expertise of the workforce in a very positive way for the mutual benefit of everyone involved.

When employees begin to buy into the improvement processes, new ideas spring from a variety of sources. For example, Servicemaster, a national corporation handling the housekeeping for Sinai Hospital, observed that another local hospital provided a flower in a small vase in each patient's room, with a "Welcome to our hospital" card signed by the housekeeper. Upon hearing about it, Sinai's housekeeping staff liked the idea and wanted to try something similar.

Around the same time, the head of Sinai's dietary department visited a different hospital when his wife had a baby. Here he noticed a little flower on each tray–a pink rose for those with a newborn girl, and a white rose for those with boys. The Sinai dietary staff became enthused with this idea, so suddenly, there was competition between the departments over who would give the patient a flower. They solved the problem by expanding the idea. New mothers receive a flower on their dietary tray, and other patients receive a flower from the housekeeping department.

(5) Fact-Based Decision Making - An un-quality organization relies on finger-pointing and blame to shift responsibility for unsuccessful deeds. A Total Quality organization applies a structured approach to problem solving as "opportunities to improve." The "TQM approach" recognizes everyone involved in the process including executive, management, workforce, suppliers, and customers, and acknowledges that they can contribute to a mutually-beneficial solution. It means understanding the processes you work in and around every day, understanding the cause of your problems, and gathering information, data on which you can base decisions for improving the process. It relies heavily on excellent team-building, communication, and interpersonal skills to develop and yield the best your people can offer. Personality conflicts and personal biases are overcome with one common focus–process improvement–with everyone lending a helping hand and no one being blamed.

The importance of planning in fact-based decision making was already clear to Larry Cox when he become Director of Material Management for St. Anthony Hospital, a 684-bed facility in Oklahoma City. As a retired Air Force officer, he had three years of direct TQM involvement with the Air Force Logistics Command, which went on to win the 1991 President's Quality Award–the federal equivalent to the Malcolm Baldrige Award.

Through various assessments, Larry found the hospital's manual material management system overtaxed and in need of process improvement. Since effective material management depends upon good databases, the first step of their strategic plan consisted of installing a computer system. To select that system, St. Anthony consulted the 14 other hospitals in their health care system. Working together in a TQM mode, they determined the requirements needed for the system. Meanwhile, teams visited the hospitals and studied their practices to help develop a "best practices" process. As Larry explains, "The idea is not to bring in a computer to automate a bad process, but to improve the process, then automate it."

Although it will take about five years for the entire strategic plan to be carried out, Larry has seen encouraging results in a very short time. The process improvements, combined with a customer-oriented approach to serving the departments, have already helped integrate the departments of the hospital, increase efficiency, and reduce material costs.

(6) Feedback - The sixth and final principle of TQM is feedback. This one principle allows the other five principles to flourish. Here, communications is key. To an engineer, it would be unthinkable to design hardware without some element of feedback. For an automobile going down the highway, feedback may be as simple as a speedometer indicating the speed at which the vehicle is moving. For a spacecraft traveling through space, unaided by man for instantaneous decision-making, feedback comes through an assortment of sensors which allow it to make decisions on its own. In manufacturing, feedback may take the form of a graph that flags the operator so a tool can be changed out, preventing production of an out-of-tolerance part. In an administrative function, feedback may take the form of a supervisor sitting next to a valued employee reviewing his annual evaluation. This one-on-one, or person-to-person, feedback is probably the most important, but seemingly the most difficult for line supervisors to accomplish.

The Albuquerque Marriott Hotel uses a Gemstone Program to provide positive feedback to its staff. Employees receive a $25.00 bonus and a blue gemstone for reducing costs or improving the way the hotel does business; pink gemstones are awarded for commendable performance, such as a life-saving act or going above the call of duty. Anyone who earns three gemstones of the same color qualifies for a reward or pay raise.

The greatest responsibility and challenge for a supervisor comes about not from managing money, facilities, or schedules, but rather from leading people to grow. Providing honest feedback, with an obvious, sincere desire to help your people improve their performance, will make you the employer of choice.

It should be noted that in many respects, TQM is nothing more than a reemphasis of basic personnel management practices. Working with employees one-on-one to develop performance goals, providing regular feedback, and offering encouragement are fundamental skills that allow managers to successfully climb the corporate ladder. At the foundation of all these skills is the ability to lead, to get people to do what they ordinarily would not have done on their own. But they do it because you lead them in a manner that inspires them to be creative and to take a chance. They view you as fair, as someone who will acknowledge their efforts and their success. Of all the departments a new employee might work for, yours becomes the one of choice.

> *You can accomplish anything you want as long as you let someone else take the credit.*

Dr. Joe Mullins

Philosophy versus Tools

When speaking to laypeople on the subject of TQM, a picture forms in my mind as to what they think TQM really is. Generally, their perceptions take on one of two forms. First, they may consider it a philosophy of management, or a guiding set of principles that allows someone to manage better. Or they may believe it to be an assortment of sophisticated statistical and measurement tools which few people use in their daily worklife, and fewer still understand. Both points of view are partially correct. There are two distinct elements to TQM—the principles of TQM and the tools.

The philosophy of Total Quality Management allows us to breach the traditional barriers that restrain executives and managers from utilizing the tremendous potential stored in each and every one of their people. This new philosophy emphasizes a few guiding principles and applies to both large and small organizations.

Following the examples of those who have implemented TQM and succeeded, one can better understand how it is possible. The essence of TQM allows us to set our expectations higher than we have in the past, to recognize and remove barriers to change, and to enable high-level managers to solicit the opinions and ideas of their associates and do something with those good ideas. To support the philosophy of TQM, we have a set of tools. These qualitative and quantitative tools allow us to better understand the way we do business. They allow us to measure improved quality along the way toward continuous improvement and recognize when we are achieving our goals of improved productivity, performance, efficiency, worklife, and eventually, improved quality. Many of these tools have existed for decades, possibly even centuries, but what makes their use unique today is our recognition that they allow us to focus on and measure what is important to us.

In manufacturing, we can easily measure a quality parameter, such as a fraction of nonconforming product that is discarded prior to customer shipping. In service companies or administrative functions; however, we cannot define the quality parameter as clearly. Applying these tools to service and administrative processes allows us to improve the majority of the work processes around us every day. We recognize quality in this new environment in reduced customer complaints and reduced reprocessing of administrative paperwork. In some instances, the simple modification of an administrative form can facilitate its use and reduce data-entry errors. In all cases, whether manufacturing or administrative/service applications of TQM, the goal is the same: "Get it right the first time."

Even excellent organizations discover the power of this philosophy and set of tools for improvement when employees are empowered to initiate change. The Albuquerque Marriott, a 410-room hotel, earned recognition as the top hotel for guest satisfaction in 1988 and 1989. Nonetheless, in 1989 the hotel started a TQM program. Shortly after attending a "quality fair," a kitchen supervisor, Anna Casau, observed that the customary breakfast garnish, a small cherry cobbler with whipped cream, frequently returned to the kitchen untouched.

Anna approached the executive chef, who asked her to track the garnish for one month to determine the cost. Anna did so, using TQM tools. The following month, Anna changed the garnish to strawberries with whipped cream and again measured the returns to the kitchen. The amount of uneaten breakfast garnish dropped dramatically–from 70 percent to less than 10 percent. Because of the price of strawberries, the process improvement didn't result in cost savings. But it did reduce waste and increase customer satisfaction–two supremely important factors in the hospitality industry.

TQM includes molding individual behavior and imparting a feeling to the employee that something positive is taking place and progress is being made. So, in contrast to philosophy driving the organization toward change, the tools oftentimes drive the philosophy at management and workforce levels within the corporation. As Schonberger explains, "regardless of the culture, techniques can mold behavior" (Schonberger, 1986). Yes, before propagating the philosophy of TQM through the organization, the application of a few simple tools at the working level can influence behavior. An example of this technique is how responsibilities previously reserved for managers are now being handled by regular employees. In TQM we call it participative management.

What Is a Process?

Webster's defines a process as a series of actions or operations that leads to a particular result. Similarly, in TQM we define a process as a series of operations linked together to provide a result that has increased value. Exhibit 2-2 illustrates a process. To the left, we put something into the process and to the right, we have an output, or a result with increased value. This increased value emerges from an exchange for resources. We most often include as resources people, equipment, material, money, and/or time. In a service company, we may have a purchase order entering a process that results in dispatching a team to repair a computer in the field. The process itself uses a person's time to review the incoming purchase order, analyze the skills needed to address this particular problem, assign the work, and then dispatch the team to do its job. This one example demonstrates how an apparently simple, routine function plays an integral role in the performance of a computer-services department.

EXHIBIT 2-2
The Process

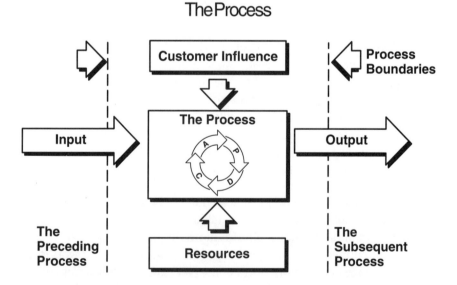

Prior to the computer repair ever being accomplished, a multitude of processes had to take place. A marketing department spread the word— advertising to inform potential consumers about the business. In addition, the staff maintains qualified personnel to accomplish the actual repair.

Therefore, before dispatching a team, the personnel department must identify the necessary qualifications for this person, advertise the position, schedule interviews, and accomplish all of the necessary paperwork so the selected candidate can become an associate of the company. Likewise, some processes are performed after the team has returned from successfully repairing the computer. These processes include invoicing the customer, posting revenues in accounting, and of course, providing feedback to the team on its performance.

So, as you can see, one single process within an organization does not function alone. Rather, it interconnects many different processes, allowing you to earn a reputation for excellent service. Factors that reinforce this view from the customer's perspective include courteous and efficient telephone personnel to receive the order, qualified and efficient repair personnel to resolve the problem, and timely invoicing with appropriate follow-up and accounting. Clearly, providing excellent customer service goes far beyond the individual in the field turning the wrench or installing a new printed circuit board. It is the smooth operation of many corporate relationships between the big "C's" and lots of little "c's" that allows the customer to conclude that you offer excellent service.

I wanted to walk through a service example here specifically because so many books on this subject focus on manufacturing examples. In manufacturing, we routinely think of the time it takes to perform an individual operation, such as installing a screw. This time, the operation-cycle time, is the accumulation and interrelationship of many steps involved in a process. These very same principles and concepts that allow us to streamline, optimize, and understand manufacturing processes apply directly to administrative and service processes as well.

To reiterate, a process is a series of operations linked together to provide a result that has increased value. We achieve this increased value in exchange for the expenditure of resources. What processes in your company add value and allow you to stay in business?

Before closing this section, I would like to mention one very important point. All processes have constraints. When designing a new process from scratch, we immediately form an impression of how to carry out this process. Then we encounter the process constraints. When performing a process, such as moving a department from one building to another, you may be asked to perform the same or improved services with fewer resources. Fewer resources may mean less floor space. If your company recently cut back personnel, your constraint may be to perform the same job with fewer people, or a reduced budget. Regardless of the reason, you confront some constraints—challenges to do more with less. Understanding the processes and successfully applying the principles and tools of TQM allows you to respond to and successfully accommodate these new challenges.

Service versus Manufacturing Companies

One aspect of quality that has always intrigued me is the lack of attention to the subject in the service arena. When recognized gurus on the topic refer to the application of quality in service companies, they typically deal with it in the following way.

They consume one hundred pages or so using case studies, hard-hitting examples, and personal experiences showing how they have helped a manufacturing company improve. Without elaboration, they go on to describe, usually in a page or so, how the same principles and tools also apply to service companies. They routinely overlook two key points, which I would like to cover here.

First, when describing process improvement we must recognize the fact that many processes typically associated with these successes are not manufacturing-related at all. Yes, statistical process control was probably used to ensure the production of a quality part on the shop floor. But other administrative and support functions are typically overlooked. Some administrative functions that immediately come to mind include contracts, personnel, and maintenance. Administrative functions that always seem to lend themselves to improvement are procurement and the processing of Engineering Change Proposals (ECPs). There, the "boiler plate" has always prompted quality professionals to unlimited opportunities for process improvement. One of the most enlightening examples I have seen is in streamlining the processing of ECPs at the U.S. Air Force Aeronautical Systems Division (ASD). There, using some simple tools of TQM (i.e. flow-charting), they reduced the time required to process ECPs by 40 percent, with the added benefit of saving 20 percent of the man-hours to accomplish the task.

"Boiler plate" usually means cutting and splicing from past contracts to yield a "standard" contract, with outdated requirements producing standardized results that are consistent with history. Inevitably, this leads to a tangled mass of verbiage. In contrast, under TQM each contractual requirement is scrutinized for quality. Genuine requirements, those insuring a certain quality product or service, must be specified and the non-requirements deleted. The best example I can think of in this area applies to government contracts. It seems so easy to add additional requirements to each new contract to overcome a fluke, or one-of-a-kind occurrence that caused problems in the past. This management-by-exception has no place in a Total Quality organization and is presently being overcome by the government's own quality initiative.

The personnel department is another support function that allows manufacturing operations to run smoothly. We have all heard the term "garbage in - garbage out" as it applies to computers. We must have good information entering the machine to produce quality results. This concept also applies to the corporate personnel function. In deploying Total Quality throughout, the personnel department becomes aware of its key role—insuring that personnel, our greatest resource, meet the quality level we desire from team members. Total Quality companies recognize that hiring a new person is a *long-term investment*. The company maintains the responsibility of selling that individual on the long-term promise of his or her affiliation. As a company moves toward Total Quality, it begins to earn a reputation for excellence and can choose from the best employee prospects. When I think of companies that have already earned such a reputation, certain names come to mind including Electronic Data Systems (EDS) in the computer services area, Sandia National Laboratories in research and development, and of course, the good name of IBM. Many people would like to work for these excellent companies or companies like them, but not everyone can. Is it your goal to work for an excellent company? Will you aid the process of transforming your company into an EDS or an IBM?

Second, manufacturing companies have a mix of service and administrative functions that allows them to produce a quality product. The orchestration of all these functions, not just the shop floor functions themselves, enables them to produce quality. I once visited a manufacturing company in El

Monte, California, where they produce electronic boxes, primarily for Department of Defense customers. After a brief introduction to their company and product line, I concluded their manufacturing operation was a "quality" operation. So what could they do next to improve their quality? Well, their accounting books disclosed that only about fifteen percent of their expenses were incurred in traditional manufacturing, shop floor activities. The balance was spent on various functions which supported manufacturing such as finance, marketing, sales, personnel, purchasing, etc. So where does this company go to improve its operations? Obviously, to where it spends 85% of its money. Manufacturing and service companies do share common service functions, but differences exist as well. These key points follow below in Exhibit 2-3 (DiPrimo), 1987.

EXHIBIT 2-3
Service versus Manufacturing Organizations

❏ **No Product with Exact Specifications**

❏ **Services Are Perishable**

❏ **Strong Customer/Client Presence**

❏ **Delivery System**

First, service companies have no product with exact specifications. Yes, they probably use some metric to tell them when they are on track, but this differs considerably from a manufactured product with critical dimensions and close tolerances. One example comes to mind from my own experience in technical consulting services, while with Booz Allen and Hamilton.

When selling a potential client on our services, we used "The Booz Allen Approach." It comprised our best effort to offer a structured methodology for problem solving. In the high technology arena, it is frequently difficult to predict what form the final product might take. So instead, we sold the client on our approach to the problem—identifying sources of information, critical decision points, etc. In doing so, we created an appreciation in the mind of our client that this was a new problem, one that had never been dealt with before. We had our arms around an approach to deal with the situation and communicated our understanding of it. The Booz Allen Approach. This is in sharp contrast to a manufacturing problem, where the results appear in a drawing beforehand and the quality of the final product is measured with calipers.

Second, services are perishable. This became quite apparent when President Reagan called for the technical expertise of this nation to be directed toward the Strategic Defense Initiative. As government research dollars shifted, the skills required for meeting the challenge changed as well. The unavailability of the technical skills necessary to build this system soon became evident; bomb designers for terrestrial systems aren't the same as the bomb designers for space systems. Special people had to be groomed to meet the technical services required for the conception and design of the new system. Today we see another shift taking place. Technical specialists who just a few years ago were immersed in defense problems are now applying their skills to environmental issues. Technical skills are perishable and not readily transferable to what may appear to be a similar problem.

The third difference applies to the area of client/customer presence. In manufacturing, we see a crate with a packing slip and invoice being received by the loading dock. Sometimes all producer/customer interaction takes place via letter and telephone with little or no direct, face-to-face contact. This differs considerably from a service organization.

Let me continue the computer service example from earlier in the book. A repair person arrives at your facility, opens the machine, evaluates the problem, proceeds to open a tool case and goes to work. All along, office personnel watch, wondering how the repair person can solve the problem so quickly, with such a complicated device. For some reason, a certain curiosity arises when equipment is opened, creating a one-on-one interaction between the service person and the customer.

This is also true if you offer a specialized technical service. Everyone in the meeting gathers around the consultant to gaze at the intricate drawings, understand every detail on the flow chart, and scrutinize every line of the computer print-out. In the services area, a real person stops by to deliver that service. The client/customer usually seizes the opportunity to ask questions, to better understand what is going on...to communicate.

The fourth contrasting factor between service and manufacturing is the delivery system involved. This extends from the discussion above on strong customer/client presence. Manufacturers commonly rely on a common carrier as the delivery system for a component. Again, this differs from the delivery of a service, where a company representative usually does the delivering. This holds true whether it involves the delivery of a computer repair service, or the presentation of a methodology for solving a complex technological problem using the Booz Allen Approach.

In conclusion, differences do exist between service and manufacturing companies. However, the same features that make the delivery of services to the client/customer something special can be applied to manufacturing projects as well. Also, it should be evident that many of the things traditionally associated with service companies are embodied within manufacturing companies, in what we call "administrative functions." Both differences and similarities exist. The understanding of these similarities and differences can help your organization apply TQM more successfully.

Chapter 3. Standards of Excellence

Malcolm Baldrige National Quality Award

When first considering a quality focus, corporate executives wrestle with the question, "What is the 'measuring stick' for quality?" While the specific answer varies from company to company, an excellent starting point is the examination criteria for the Malcolm Baldrige National Quality Award.

The Malcolm Baldrige National Quality Improvement Act of 1987, Public Law 100-107, signed by President Reagan on August 20, 1987, establishes an annual United States National Quality Award. The purposes of the Award are to promote quality awareness, to recognize quality achievements of U.S. companies, and to publicize successful quality strategies.

The Award formally recognizes companies that attain preeminent quality leadership and permits these companies to publicize and advertise their awards. It encourages other companies to improve their quality management practices in order to compete more effectively for future awards. It develops and publishes Award criteria that will also serve as quality improvement guidelines for use by U.S. companies. Furthermore, it widely disseminates non-proprietary information about the quality strategies of the Award recipients. It gets the word out that quality is achievable.

The Malcolm Baldrige National Award Criteria form the basis for making Awards and providing feedback to applicants. In addition, they have three other important national purposes: to help elevate quality standards and expectations; to facilitate communication and sharing among and within organizations of all types based upon a common understanding of key quality requirements; and to serve as a working tool for planning, training, and assessment.

The Award Criteria are directed toward dual results-oriented goals: to project key requirements for delivering ever-improving value to customers, while at the same time to maximize the overall productivity and effectiveness of the delivering organization.

The 1992 Award Criteria are built upon the same seven-category framework and use the same approach as in 1991. However, numerous changes have been made to improve clarity and strengthen key themes. Major changes include a reduction in the number of examination categories from 32 to 28, and a reallocation of point values to provide overall balance and place more emphasis on results. But *Customer Focus and Satisfaction* still occupies the lion's share of the total points.

An expanded introductory section in the 1992 instruction booklet, entitled "Description of the 1992 Award Criteria," is provided to enhance the educational value of the Criteria for wider usage–training, self-assessment, and design of quality systems, as well as actual Award applications. This is consistent with my own personal experience; more companies, both large and small, are using the criteria as a training and self-assessment tool. Exhibit 3-1 reinforces this point. Although the total number of applications, site visits, and Awards has remained fairly constant, the number of criteria booklets shipped by the National Institute of Standards and Technology has increased twenty times since the first Award year, 1988. In Japan only five or six companies typically apply for the Deming Prize each year, a 41-year-old quality contest.

Up to two Malcolm Baldrige National Quality Awards may be given annually in each of three categories: (1) manufacturing companies or subsidiaries; (2) service companies or subsidiaries; and (3) small businesses. Fewer than two Awards may be given in a category if the high standards of the Award Program are not met. Any for-profit businesses located in the United States or its territories may apply for the Award. Subsidiaries—divisions or business units of larger companies—are eligible if they primarily serve either the public or businesses other than the parent company. For companies engaged in both services and manufacturing, the larger percentage of sales determines the classification. For purposes of the Award, small businesses are defined as independently-owned businesses with fewer than 500 full-time employees.

EXHIBIT 3-1
Malcolm Baldrige National Quality Award
Selected Data on Applicants

Application Year	Description	Manufacturing	Service	Small Business	Totals
1988	Booklets Shipped				12,000*
	Applications	45	9	12	66
	Site Visits	10	2	1	13
	Awards	2	0	1	3
1989	Booklets Shipped				65,000*
	Applications	23	6	11	40
	Site Visits	8	2	0	10
	Awards	2	0	0	2
1990	Booklets Shipped				180,000*
	Applications	45	18	34	97
	Site Visits	6	3	3	12
	Awards	2	1	1	4
1991	Booklets Shipped				235,000*
	Applications	38	21	47	106
	Site Visits	9	5	5	19
	Awards	2	0	1	3

*Denotes figures rounded to nearest thousand.

Source: Malcolm Baldrige National Quality Award
   National Institute for Standards and Technology. April 1992.

Examination Process

The Malcolm Baldrige National Quality Award Examination applies to manufacturing and service businesses of any size. The examination permits evaluation of the strengths and areas for improvement in the applicant's quality systems and shows their results. It addresses all aspects of quality improvement using the following seven evaluation categories shown in Exhibit 3-2.

EXHIBIT 3-2
Malcolm Baldrige National Quality Award Seven Evaluation Categories

1.0 Leadership

2.0 Information and Analysis

3.0 Strategic Quality Planning

4.0 Human Resource Development and Management

5.0 Management of Process Quality

6.0 Quality and Operational Results

7.0 Customer Focus and Satisfaction

Each category is assigned a number of points totaling up to 1,000. Exhibit 3-3 shows the examination items, along with the point allocations. It's not surprising that Category 7.0, *Customer Satisfaction*, carries the most weight in the examination process (300 points). Its nearest competitor, *Quality and Operational Results*, carries 180 points.

The **Leadership** Category examines senior executives' personal leadership and involvement in creating and sustaining a customer focus with clear and visible quality values. Judges also examine how the quality values are integrated into the company's management system and reflected in the manner in which the company addresses its public responsibilities. In the country of Mexico, public responsibility to the environment has become so important that it warrants its own examination category within their quality award system.

EXHIBIT 3-3

Malcolm Baldrige National Quality Award
Examination Categories, Items and Point Values

1992 Examination Categories /Items		Maximum Points
1.0 Leadership		**90**
1.1 Senior Executive Leadership	45	
1.2 Management for Quality	25	
1.3 Public Responsibility	20	
2.0 Information and Analysis		**80**
2.1 Scope and Management of Quality and Performance Data and Information	15	
2.2 Competitive Comparisons and Benchmarks	25	
2.3 Analysis and Uses of Company-Level Data	40	
3.0 Strategic Quality Planning		**60**
3.1 Strategic Quality and Company Performance Planning Process	35	
3.2 Quality and Performance Plans	25	
4.0 Human Resources Development and Management		**150**
4.1 Human Resource Management	20	
4.2 Employee Involvement	40	
4.3 Employee Education and Training	40	
4.4 Employee Performance and Recognition	25	
4.5 Employee Well-Being and Morale	25	
5.0 Management of Process Quality		**140**
5.1 Design and Introduction of Quality Products and Services	40	
5.2 Process Management–Product and Service Production and Delivery Processes	35	
5.3 Process Management–Business Processes and Support Services	30	
5.4 Supplier Quality	20	
5.5 Quality Assessment	15	
6.0 Quality and Operational Results		**180**
6.1 Product and Service Quality Results	75	
6.2 Company Operational Results	45	
6.3 Business Process and Support Service Results	25	
6.4 Supplier Quality Results	35	
7.0 Customer Focus and Satisfaction		**300**
7.1 Customer Relationship Management	65	
7.2 Commitment to Customers	15	
7.3 Customer Satisfaction Determination	35	
7.4 Customer Satisfaction Results	75	
7.5 Customer Satisfaction Comparison	75	
7.6 Future Requirements and Expectations of Customers	35	
Total Points		**1000**

Source: Dept. of Commerce, 1991

The **Information and Analysis** Category examines the scope, validity, analysis, management, and use of data and information to drive quality excellence and improve competitive performance. Also examined is the adequacy of the company's data, information, and analysis system to support improvement of the organization's customer focus, products, services, and internal operations.

The **Strategic Quality Planning** Category assesses the company's planning process and the way key quality requirements integrate into overall business planning. It also reviews the company's short-and longer-term plans, evaluating how quality performance requirements are deployed to all work units. The implementation process for TQM described in this book considers strategic planning as an integral part.

The **Human Resource Development and Management** Category examines the key elements of how the company develops and realizes the full potential of the work force to pursue quality and performance objectives. Additionally, reviewers evaluate the company's efforts to build and maintain an environment for quality excellence conducive to full participation and personal and organizational growth.

The **Management of Process Quality** Category considers the systematic processes the company uses to pursue ever-higher quality and company performance. Topics include the key elements of process management, such as design, management of process quality for all work units and suppliers, systematic quality improvement, and quality assessment.

The **Quality and Operational Results** Category encompasses the company's quality levels and improvement trends in quality, company operational performance and supplier quality. Reviewers also consider current quality and performance levels relative to those of competitors.

The **Customer Focus and Satisfaction** Category evaluates the company's relationships with customers and its knowledge of customer requirements and the key quality factors that determine marketplace competitiveness. Judges rate the company's methods of determining customer satisfaction, current trends and levels of satisfaction and compare these results to the competition.

Site Visits

At least four members of the Board of Examiners review each application. High-scoring applicants are selected for site visits, made by one or more teams of examiners. A panel of nine judges from the Board of Examiners reviews all data and information and recommends Award recipients. Award recommendations are based not only upon scores applicants receive on the written examination, but also upon the judges' assessment of overall strengths and areas for improvement as determined from site visits. The recommendations of the judges are final and not subject to appeal. All applicants receive written feedback, summarizing strengths and areas for improvement relative to the Award examination categories.

The primary objectives of the site visits are to verify the information provided in the Application Report and to clarify issues and questions raised during a review of the Report. During site visits, applicants make presentations, and examiner teams conduct interviews and review data and pertinent records. Most visits last two to three days. Site visit teams prepare reports for submission to the judges. During site visits, applicants may be asked to provide data for inclusion in this report. Additional information or data will not be accepted from the applicant once site visits are completed, unless specifically requested by the Board of Examiners. Applicants selected for site visits will be asked to authorize a review of their tax status regarding filing of tax returns, payment of taxes, and absence of criminal offenses and fraud. This information ensures suitability of the applicant as a national Award winner.

Awards

Awards are presented each year in November. Award recipients receive a medal contained in a crystal base. The medal bears the inscriptions, "Malcolm Baldrige National Quality Award" and "The Quest for Excellence." Recipients may publicize and advertise receipt of their Award, provided they agree to share information about their successful quality strategies with other American organizations.

Those Who Succeed

On October 29, 1991 Vice President Quayle and Secretary of Commerce Mosbacher presented the Malcolm Baldrige National Quality Award to three companies—Marlow Industries, Solectron, and Zytec Corporation. These three companies prevailed from among 106 applicants.

Marlow Industries

Marlow Industries exemplifies the idea of a good business becoming even better. This Dallas-based firm manufactures customized thermoelectric (TE) coolers—small, solid-state electronic devices that regulate the temperature of electronic equipment. What began as a five-person operation in 1973 now employs 160 people and has total annual sales of $12 million. Marlow is the third small company to receive the Baldrige Award.

Though already a world leader in manufacturing TE coolers, in 1987 Marlow initiated a TQM program. Since that time, employee productivity has increased 10 percent annually; the time between design and production has been trimmed; and the cost of scrap, rework, and other nonconformance errors has been reduced by nearly one-half.

At Marlow Industries the emphasis on quality begins with the CEO and President, Raymond Marlow. His direct involvement encourages employees to participate in the continuous improvement process. All TQM Council sessions include worker representatives. Monthly company-wide meetings review company performance, recognize employees for quality contributions, review quality values and enforce the team concept.

Training programs, an average of 32 hours per year for each employee, impart the skills required for achieving the expected standards. All workers, including the temporary employees, receive quality-awareness training; and the entire permanent work force has completed initial courses in statistical problem solving. Three-fifths of these people have undergone more comprehensive training in the use of quality tools.

Since over 90 percent of Marlow's products are custom designed to meet specific requirements, customer satisfaction is a key factor. To ensure a clear focus on the customers' needs, the company has developed an exhaustive system for obtaining feedback—from several types of surveys to quarterly meetings with major clients. This emphasis on quality has enhanced

Marlow's good reputation in manufacturing. Since 1988 the firm has won six major quality awards from customers; and in 1990, its top 10 customers rated the quality of Marlow TE coolers at 100 percent.

Solectron

Founded in 1977, Solectron has grown from a small assembly job shop to an employer of 2,100 people working at five sites in California. About 80 percent of the business comes from assembling printed circuit boards. The rest is derived from a variety of activities, such as software packaging, disk duplication, and design and testing services.

At Solectron, customer needs drive results. Each week customers are surveyed and the results compiled into a customer satisfaction index. The CEO, Dr. Winston Chen, and other top executives review the index at one of their three weekly meetings on quality-related issues.

In addition, each Solectron customer is supported by two teams that help ensure quality performance and on-time delivery. A project planning team works with customers in planning, scheduling, defining requirements, and lead time. A total quality control team evaluates production weekly to prevent potential problems and identify ways to improve processes.

The concept of continuous improvement is embedded in Solectron's corporate culture. Every department uses Statistical Process Control (SPC) regularly to track performance of the machines. Each day the division quality managers and the corporate quality director track and review the results. Since 1987 the average product rejection rate has improved by 50 percent.

Solectron has tangible evidence that the quality improvement efforts pay off. Over the past ten years it has won 37 superior performance awards—10 of those in 1990. But perhaps even more rewarding is the feedback from the customers. After a recent quality audit, a major customer rated Solectron as the "best contract manufacturer of electronic assemblies in the U.S."

Zytec Corporation

This Minnesota firm focused on quality, service, and value from its start in 1984. With 748 workers, Zytec Corporation has become the fifth largest U.S. manufacturer of AC to DC power supplies. Ninety percent of the revenue is derived from sales of customized power supplies. In addition, Zytec repairs cathode-ray tube monitors and power supplies.

On-going improvement efforts have brought about meaningful results. Since 1988 Zytec has improved manufacturing yields by 50 percent; reduced the manufacturing cycle time by 26 percent; reduced the design cycle by 50 percent; and decreased product costs by 30-40 percent. Zytec attributes much of this success to its quality improvement efforts, organized around the concepts of W. Edwards Deming.

Zytec employees receive 72 hours of quality-related training, with a strong emphasis on analytical and problem-solving methods. These tools become invaluable to employees, as their authority and responsibilities grow. To maintain this momentum, an innovative employee evaluation and reward system, the Multi-Functional Employee program, rewards production workers for improving their knowledge and acquiring new job skills.

A "Management by Planning" process involves employees from all 33 departments in setting the long-term and annual improvement goals. At an annual two-day meeting, 150 employees review and critique five-year plans. Selected customers and suppliers are also invited to scrutinize the plan, leading to refinement. Based on this input, Zytec executives finalize the long-term strategic plan and set broad corporate objectives to guide quality planning. At this point, teams in each department develop goals to support the objectives.

A data-driven company, Zytec develops measurable criteria for evaluating performance at all levels. In addition, Zytec benchmarks competitors' products and services to obtain a clear picture of what it takes to achieve excellence in all areas—from employee involvement to supplier management.

> *"Quality management is not just a strategy. It must be a new style of working, even a new style of thinking. A dedication to quality and excellence is more than good business. It is way of life, giving something back to society, offering your best to others."*

(Dept. of Commerce, 1992)

George Bush

For more information on the Malcolm Baldrige National Quality Award, call or write:

> Malcolm Baldrige National Quality Award
> National Institute of Standards and Technology
> 5th Floor, Bldg 101
> Gaithersburg, Maryland 20899
> (301) 975-2036

Quality Recognition at the State Level

To date, fifteen states have a recognition system for quality, and the list is growing. My home state, New Mexico, will introduce its quality award during the University of New Mexico's Fourth Annual TQM Forum, scheduled in February 1993. Many state-level award systems, like New Mexico's, closely resemble the Malcolm Baldrige Criteria. Let's look at one example in detail.

The New York State (NYS) award program was announced by Governor Mario M. Cuomo at a press conference on June 27, 1991. Called the Excelsior Award, it is based on the Malcolm Baldrige Criteria, but with two important differences. First, it places heavy emphasis on labor-management cooperation; customer satisfaction is equally weighed with human resource excellence. And second, New York State has three unique applications with common criteria: Private Sector Application, Public Sector Application, and Education Sector Application.

The first Excelsior Award winners were announced at an Awards Dinner on May 21, 1992. The two Award recipients in the private sector were the Motorola Plant in Elma, NY and Albany International, Press Fabrics Division in East Greenbush, NY. The New York State Police won the public sector Award. And in the education application area, the Kenmore-Town of Tonawanda School District received the honor.

> *"Our winners speak the language of quality, one which all of New York's institutions need to speak fluently. All the sectors of our society and economy depend on each other for high quality—from schools providing well-educated graduates, to companies producing world-class quality goods, to governments efficiently providing necessary public services."*
>
> Governor Cuomo
> May 7, 1992

Other Quality Recognition Systems

We also have a United States Federal Government level award for quality. Modeled after the Malcolm Baldrige National Quality Award, the President's Award for Quality is administered by the Federal Quality Institute in Washington, D.C. Panels of examiners from both the private and public sectors evaluate an agency's application and judge its merits through on-site assessments. Twenty agencies have been awarded the Quality Improvement Prototype Award to date, a precursor to the President's Award. The winners serve as models for all federal agencies, and their successful practices are being adapted across government.

ISO 9000

If you perform work for the Department of Defense or overseas industries, you will undoubtedly come into contact with the International Standards Organization quality systems, known as ISO 9000. These systems resemble those of the Malcolm Baldrige National Quality Award, but with a slightly different emphasis. Prepared in 1987 by the Technical Committee ISO/TC 176 on Quality Assurance, the ISO standards were developed to standardize national and international quality requirements. Like the Malcolm Baldrige Award, ISO 9000 has an independent review process which relies on rigorous evaluation criteria. Unlike the Baldrige Award, it is not an Award/Recognition system per se. Rather, it qualifies a company's quality system to sell directly to countries within the European Common Market without the added expense of having an independent inspector review the quality of the product or service. As Dan Meckstroth, an economist for a manufacturer's trade group puts it, "If you win the Baldrige, you get a pat on the back...ISO 9000 may mean preserving your market in Europe."

An international committee organized the ISO documents into three broad categories. ISO 9001 applies to engineering or construction-type firms and manufacturers; ISO 9002 pertains to the chemical and process industries, where product requirements exist as an established design or specification; and ISO 9003 concerns small shops or divisions within an organization which inspect and test products.

When applying for ISO certification, a firm requests an accredited third-party to review its overall quality system. ISO auditors study the processes to certify that the firm's quality system meets ISO requirements. The company's quality system is then "certified." Unannounced surveillance audits verify that the quality system continues to meet registration requirements. If a nonconformance is raised, the burden of proof rests with the auditor, not the company.

In choosing a registrar, quality directors must understand that not all ISO certificates are recognized by an official government agency. So it's important to select a registrar with experience in your industry and accreditation in the part of the world you export to. The National Accreditation of Certification Bodies (NACB) publishes a Directory of Accredited Certification Bodies to help with the selection process.

This relatively new system is gaining momentum with multi-national companies in the United States. More than 35 countries worldwide and the U.S. Department of Defense have adopted the ISO 9000 series of standards and the third-party audit system. Most of the people implementing an ISO quality system have expressed very favorable opinions with regard to ISO 9000 certification.

> *"World-class quality begins at home. It should not be an export commodity, but an undifferentiated performance standard for every neighbor and nation."*

Robert V. Caine
President
ASQC

For more information on the ISO 9000 series of standards, call or write:

> National Center for Standards and Certification Information (NCSCI)
> National Institute of Standards and Technology
> TRF Bldg. #411, Room A163
> Gaithersburg, Maryland 20899
> (301) 975-4040

They can suggest whom to call for specific information about the latest in standards for the 9000 series.

Chapter 4. TQM Implementation

Overview: Implementation Approach

Exhibit 4-1 provides an overview to the Five-Phase Approach™ to implementing TQM in your corporation. Subsequent chapters describe each phase in detail as a logical sequence of events, or milestones. Many of the questions that may surface in the interim will be addressed in reviewing the implementation schedule in Chapter 10. The schedule identifies interrelationships that must be maintained throughout implementation to insure a smooth transformation from your current status to your goal for the future.

This Approach Is Unique

Many approaches have been used to implement corporate-wide change, but this approach is unique because of several aspects in its content and delivery. They are:

1. addressing tough issues and
2. describing costs and rewards of implementing change .

Some of the tough issues I address in this approach include management commitment and resistance to change. Many executives talk about management commitment, but few take on the challenge of describing in detail what they must do to make corporate-wide change, the successful implementation of TQM, a reality. The absence of this important topic in any

EXHIBIT 4-1
Overview: Five-Phase Approach™ to Implementation

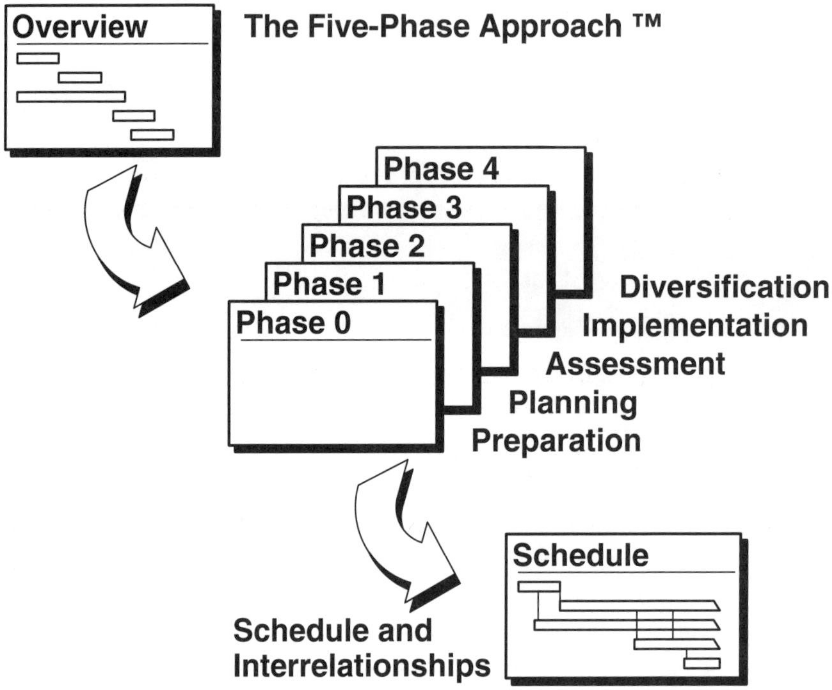

Overview | The Five-Phase Approach ™

Phase 4 — Diversification
Phase 3 — Implementation
Phase 2 — Assessment
Phase 1 — Planning
Phase 0 — Preparation

Schedule and Interrelationships

Schedule

implementation strategy has time and time again lulled executives into a false sense of security, a belief that they are moving toward TQM when in reality, they are setting themselves up for failure with many adverse consequences to follow. Another tough issue relates to resistance to change. Before agreeing to implement TQM, corporate executives must be aware of resistance-to-change issues and accept the commitment of addressing those inevitable challenges before giving the final approval to implement TQM. Ignoring this can postpone a corporate thrust toward TQM and, at worst, catch corporate executives off-guard enough times so that TQM is scrapped altogether.

Next we have the issue of costs and rewards of implementing TQM. The success stories described in previous chapters shed light on several of the successful implementations of TQM: those who, undaunted by the challenges of their respective industries, rose above the rubble to recapture lost markets amidst tough competition. A careful review and analysis of these examples will help us develop our own expectations for results. We want to recognize if we are on track. A commonly overlooked area in these successful corporate transformations is the cost of implementing a corporate-wide quality focus.

I once had a conversation with a member of the government's Senior Executive Service (SES) on implementation in his organization. Although not an expert on the subject, he had taken several introductory courses in TQM. As I went through my outline of how TQM is implemented, he stopped me when I came to the section on Resources. "What's this?" he exclaimed, "I thought quality was free," a popular phrase first used by Philip Crosby, a leader in the U.S. quality movement (Crosby, 1984). I then explained that quality is better than free; you can make money on it, but there is a cash flow problem. Like the student attending classes at a local university, the executive makes the commitment of time and money so he can reap the rewards of that investment in the future. The student's return on investment for a college degree may be a better job at higher wages or greater prestige. The rewards for implementing TQM are reduced costs (as the quality focus becomes part of your day-to-day manner of doing business), increased customer retention, improved employee pride in workmanship, and increased market share. Quality is better than free, you can make money on it. But you, as a corporate leader, must be willing to make the up-front investment of time and money.

> *Quality is better than free, you can make money on it, but there is a cash flow problem.*
>
> Joseph R. Jablonski

Challenge of Change

You may be asking yourself, "If there is an investment of time and money involved with implementing TQM, why bother?" This is a good question. The decision to implement TQM is frequently based on two reasons, neither of which require an in-depth economic analysis. CEOs usually decide to "take the plunge" because: (1) they recognize that there is something to be gained, or (2) they have no choice.

The first category of CEOs represents the visionaries. They may have just returned from a professional conference, reviewed a trade publication, or been prompted by a competitor's improved position in an area that had previously been reserved for their company alone. Whatever the reason, as special leaders, these individuals recognize TQM as the mechanism for recapturing lost ground, reviving old markets, and creating new ones. These executives see TQM as an opportunity that doesn't require in-depth cost justifications or a myriad of subordinate presentations. If you decide you fall into this category, you should be applauded, because you represent one of the chosen few. With a minimum of information, you take on the important challenges of corporate-wide change on the feeling, the faith, that your company will benefit.

Everyone else changes the way they do business because they have to. If you feel you fall into this category, join the club. You represent the majority. Sometimes valued customers with enough leverage to compel an executive to change may have already been bitten by the TQM bug and realize the power in this new initiative. One of the most inspiring examples of this situation is the Motorola Corp. They made a tough decision that has become the focus of much debate. They require all of their suppliers eligible for the Malcolm Baldrige Award to sign a statement as to their intent to compete. They are, in fact, challenging their suppliers to take on stringent standards and compete head-to-head for the most prestigious of quality awards in this country. In exchange for this commitment, their suppliers become part of a winning team with proven success. I believe Motorola's leadership-by-example initiative is a good approach to follow.

In another instance, companies may decide to implement TQM because they have gotten so bad at what they do, they feel they have no choice. In this case, an analogy can be drawn between a troubled company and an alcoholic. Like the corporate executive, the alcoholic suddenly realizes that in order to survive and eventually prosper, he must change his ways. Anything short of revolutionary change is inadequate and will eventually lead him back to his old, bad habits. Unlike the alcoholic, the corporation can remove any resemblance of permanent biological damage that might be associated with the company's old way of doing business. Like an alcoholic, the corporation must continually be reformed, the new-found focus toward quality restated again and again, and an aggressive personalized plan for self-improvement adopted. Generally initiated by a catalyst, this is not a gradual change. Consider this example. During an annual physical a family physician suggests the patient lose a few pounds and cut back on consumption of salt and red meat. Statistically, most people ignore this advice and return year after year to hear the same recommendation. However, if this individual has a heart attack, suddenly the physician's advice takes on new importance. The fear of death inspires most of us to take immediate action.

Not all industry competitors have the luxury of deciding whether or not they will implement TQM in their business. However, we all, consciously or unconsciously, recognize that the important decisions we make today will either insure our competitive posture into the next century, or place the final nail in the coffin.

Existing Organizational Structure

To successfully implement TQM in any corporation, you must first recognize its existing hierarchy. Later, in Chapter 6, I show how to transform that structure into the team that will enable TQM to succeed. A typical organizational hierarchy consists of three levels: (1) Executive, (2) Management, and (3) Workforce. A fourth entity, Key Executives, is also included as a subset of the Executive level. A description of each level within the organization follows below.

(1) Executive management includes those top-level managers who make up the top two layers of management within the corporation. Executive management begins with the Chief Executive Officer (CEO), and/or President, and the layer below. This second layer may include Directors or Vice Presidents (V.P.'s). In either case, this second layer of executive management maintains responsibility over functional areas within the organization. Key Executives make up a small portion of all executive management. This small cadre of individuals is routinely consulted first on important issues confronting the organization.

Commitment forms the foundation of any successful quality process. Leadership is the key to promoting commitment. Leaders should be charismatic, inspirational and flexible–especially with regard to those they manage. Effective leaders inspire others to create and manage change, to take responsibility and listen in ways which initiate a sustainable quality process. W. Edwards Deming is frequently quoted as saying the large amount of problems in an organization is the direct responsibility and result of top management. Therefore, management, via a strong commitment, maintains responsibility for putting in place the systems which will allow TQM to flourish.

(2) Management represents people who supervise the workforce (directly or indirectly) and insure the completion of short-term organizational responsibilities. First-line supervisors are included here, as the lowest echelon of management.

(3) The workforce includes those individuals involved in the day-to-day activities of supporting the organization's function. If the organization is in the business of producing widgets, the workforce processes orders, turns wrenches, responds to customer complaints, packages and ships the product.

TQM applies to everyone. People directly involved in a process pinpoint snags in a system which might never occur to management. For example, at General Electric (G.E.), Syracuse, secretaries recognized the need to standardize the font cartridges and formats used for various kinds of correspondence. In this large organization, memos and notices flow back and forth among different managers. The secretaries realized that developing a standard operating procedure would eliminate the inordinate amount of time being wasted reformatting these internal documents. Now when managers exchange correspondence, the secretaries simply insert a disk in their machine and make the necessary changes. As empowered employees, the secretaries recognized the unnecessary time and effort involved in the process and felt comfortable suggesting and initiating the improvements. Top management creates the environment which allows this behavior to become possible.

Five-Phase Approach™ to Implementation

The following five phases are necessary for the successful implementation of TQM in your company:

Phase 0: Preparation

Phase 1: Planning

Phase 2: Assessment

Phase 3: Implementation

Phase 4: Diversification

Exhibit 4-2 will help you understand their relative sequence of occurrence and interrelationships. As you can see, Phase 0 is unique in that it has a definite beginning and end. This differs from the other phases, which evolve over time and go on continuously.

EXHIBIT 4-2
Five-Phase Approach™ to Implementation

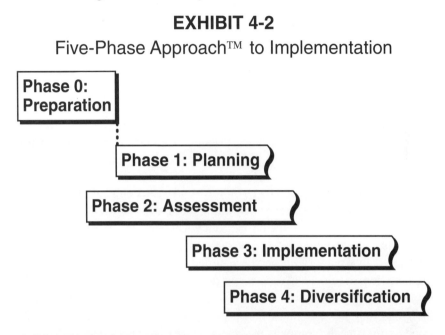

Successful implementation of TQM begins with Phase 0, Preparation. It is termed Phase 0 because it actually precedes a building process involving the organization's Key Executives, with the aid of a professional facilitator. Here, the Key Executives develop the organization's vision statement, set corporate goals and objectives, and draft policy in direct support of the corporate strategic plan. Phase 0 concludes with a commitment of resources necessary to plan the implementation of TQM.

Planning, Phase 1, lays the foundation for the process of change within the organization. Here, individuals who will make up the Corporate Council use the statements developed during the Preparation Phase and begin the meticulous planning process. Once formed, the Corporate Council develops the implementation plan, commits resources and makes it a reality. The planning process relies on inputs from all subsequent phases to help guide its implementation and evolution.

Assessment, Phase 2, involves the exchange of information necessary to support the preparation, planning, implementation and diversification phases. It consists of surveys, evaluations, questionnaires and interviews throughout the organization at all levels, as well as self-evaluations assessing individual and group perceptions of the organization's strengths and weaknesses. An important ingredient in any successful quality process is input from the big "C,", the external customer. In Phase 2, this channel of communication is created and/or strengthened.

Phase 3 is Implementation. Here, the investments made during the previous phases pay off. A well-defined training initiative for managers and the workforce begins. With full support from the Corporate Council, Process Action Teams (PATs) are chartered to evaluate and improve processes and implement change.

The final phase, Phase 4, is Diversification. Accomplishing Phase 0 (Preparation) through Phase 3 (Implementation) provides the organization with a substantial knowledge base. Policy has been defined, objections to change have been overcome, and success stories may already be reported by PATs. At this point, with newly acquired experience, other parts of the organization should be invited to participate. These others may include subordinate organizations, strategic business units, subsidiaries, off-site divisions, suppliers, vendors, or various departments within the organization. At this time the company may elect to share its experiences with others by networking through professional associations, local community groups or other interested parties.

At this point, if I were conducting a workshop on implementing TQM, I would ask the audience to pull out a clean piece of paper and draw two lines, as shown in Exhibit 4-3. The vertical line forms two columns. The horizontal line underscores the headings for these two columns. The heading on the left is titled "Done" and the heading on the right is "2-Be-Done." I would ask them to keep this sheet of paper handy throughout the workshop and fill in the two columns as we proceed through the details of the five-phase implementation process. Items in the "Done" column give us credit for what we've accomplished to date. Steps that still need "2-Be-Done" are listed in the right-hand column, which eventually becomes the organization's implementation schedule in Chapter 10.

EXHIBIT 4-3
Done and 2-Be-Done Lists

Done	*"2-Be-Done"*
○ *Decision to consider TQM*	○ *Assess need for consultant*
○ *Key Executive Training*	

Top Management Commitment — A Definition

When describing a company's commitment to change, all too often the person at the top fails to recognize the meaning of top management commitment. This major point is overlooked so often that I find it necessary to define precisely what top management commitment means.

Top management commitment is a commitment of corporate resources, including the executive's own time, to the improvement process. In fact, substantial amounts of executive time, particularly that of the CEO, are necessary to successfully implement TQM. Committing a subordinate's time and corporate funds to this initiative is not enough. Both management and the workforce assess the importance of priorities in terms of where the CEO spends the majority of his or her time. It was said best by Peter F. Drucker, a recognized management expert: "Everything degenerates into work" (Drucker, 1974). Yes, that even applies to the person at the top.

Early in Phase 0, management spends time defining the organization's vision statement, detailing corporate goals, outlining policy and making that all-important decision to proceed into the planning phase. Although accomplished along with other senior executives, the active, hands-on participation of the senior executive is essential. These results continue into the planning process, where the CEO creates and leads the Corporate Council, using his or her leadership to remove barriers which would otherwise make the responsibilities across an organization's functional boundaries irreconcilable. The person at the top must routinely voice support and enthusiasm for TQM, play a decisive role in recognizing contributors to the implementation process, participate in manager training, and create a proactive, positive image of TQM in the minds of everyone in the organization. Just as the company demonstrates TQM prior to expecting others to do it in the Diversification Phase, the CEO should also demonstrate TQM prior to expecting it of his or her people. You lead by example.

Leadership by example was demonstrated when Johnson & Johnson decided to act on environmental issues and become a world leader in protecting the environment and the people inhabiting it. The company established a pilot program, "The Model Environmental Program," at Ethicon, a division manufacturing suture and mechanical devices. The CEO, Ralph Larson, vowed to lead in the environmental initiative and imparted this enthusiasm to his personnel. The program contains three primary initiatives: technical, associate, and community. One technical project involved spending $30 million to convert the CFC-fluorocarbon sterilizers to non-CFC sterilizers. Though cheaper alternatives exist, Johnson & Johnson is more concerned with the long-term effects on the environment than short-term economics.

A recent community project by Ethicon focused on an elementary school at East San Jose, in an underprivileged section of Albuquerque. Ethicon donated money and time as their staff joined teachers and students to work on environmental projects. They have planted a huge garden, with the aim of teaching students about ecology. They have also started a beautification project, eliminating gang graffiti and dressing up the courtyard with plants and trees. As a result of this direct involvement in the community, Ethicon sees the children becoming interested in careers in these areas. As government regulations for corporations continue to expand, our country will need more environmental engineers and industrial hygiene and safety specialists. By introducing children to these concepts at an early age, Johnson & Johnson is helping to ensure that the children of today will be prepared for the jobs of tomorrow.

Quality companies in America are prepared to account for the long-term implications of their decisions. Ethicon is merely one example.

What if the CEO Isn't Committed?

This one topic has been the source of great frustration for me, personally. At one time, if confronted by an uncommitted CEO, I would have thrown up my hands and said, "Let's just forget it and part as friends right now." Unfortunately, life isn't that simple, and there are many good reasons to pursue TQM, even if certain individuals are not sold on the idea. Although an uncommitted CEO dictates failure for TQM as a corporate-wide initiative, this does not mean the pursuit of Total Quality is impossible for others in the organization. However, certain limits must be understood.

We have all seen examples of Total Quality at some level within our company. These examples of excellence may include a division, department, or section. The most obvious indicators that such a special entity exists within our own company are as follows. Everyone works hard; they're challenged; they appreciate the opportunity to excel; and everyone wants to become part of that group. They're winners. The group leader possesses unique management skills which allow him or her to practice the principles and philosophy of Total Quality, even though this individual may have had no formal training in this area. The leader may send employees to training, special instruction to enhance their ability to work as a team and improve internal processes. We have here an excellent example of Total Quality in action.

Several years ago a core group of people employed by one company became enthused with the concepts of TQM, despite management's refusal to spend the time and money required for developing a formal program. So those who really wanted to use TQM methods worked together, fostering a process improvement attitude. They sent PAT teams into the factory to talk with the workers and review their processes. Then they created a data base of all process improvement activities going on, to avoid duplication of effort. They found that by talking to others involved in similar improvement efforts, they could learn short cuts. They gained knowledge and insight from each other's experiences.

Granted, without top management commitment you're not going to get a full-blown TQM process going, but you can get a grass-roots movement, where people learn to use the tools and apply them in their own work situations. Even without a formally approved TQM process, a group of people can meet together and figure out ways to solve a problem. Then they can approach their managers and say not only, "We have a problem here," but also, "And here's how I suggest we correct it." That's the good news!

The not-so-good news is that's where it ends. The supervisor can directly influence that group's ability to perform and improve processes within their own domain. Difficulties come into play when supervisors try to improve processes, or portions of processes, outside their immediate area of responsibility that effect their results. An example in purchasing comes to mind. You may recognize the need for a new piece of equipment to significantly enhance the throughput of your department and be ready to use it at a moment's notice. However, if the purchasing department still operates under the "business as usual" philosophy, it could take six months to receive such an order. So you're stuck. You must then have a higher level of support and recognize the individual limitations in making Total Quality happen.

Chapter 5. Phase 0: Preparation

Decision to Consider TQM

The most important phase in the implementation process is Phase 0. It is here where corporate Key Executives decide if they will consider the benefits afforded by a TQM program. They obtain initial training, evaluate the need for an outside consultant, develop the organization's vision statement and corporate goals, draft corporate policy, commit initial resources, and communicate. The sequence of these events includes the ten steps described in Exhibit 5-1. The steps do not imply a span of time for each milestone; they merely denote the logical sequence of events one would follow to successfully accomplish Phase 0. Chapter 10 offers a duration for each milestone and describes the precise interrelationship of the various milestones. In contrast to the other four phases, Phase 0 has a definite beginning and ending point.

EXHIBIT 5-1
Phase 0: Preparation

△ **Decision to Consider TQM**
 △ **Key Executive Training**
  △ **Assess Need for Consultant**
   △ **Select Consultant**
    △ **Strategic Planning**
     △ Vision Statement
      △ Corporate Goals
       △ **Corporate Quality Policy**
        △ **Corporate Communication**
         △ **Decision to Proceed**

The first step is making a decision to consider implementing TQM. This decision can range from "let's do it" to "let's consider implementing TQM." Some Key Executives become inspired by the successes of a competitor; others are directed to implement a quality program by a major customer. At Jaynes Corporation, a construction company, the catalyst for formalizing their quality process came from customer inquiries on Jaynes's TQM process. Before this occurred, their focus on employee welfare and a desire to reduce costs put in place many features of a Total Quality process. At Wal-Mart, a vendor partner provided the first introduction to a Total Quality process. In the U.S. health care industry, the Joint Commission on Accreditation of Healthcare Organizations (JCHAO) has mandated that hospitals wishing to be accredited must institute a Total Quality process (Continuous Quality Improvement) within the next few years. Let's look into some of these examples in greater detail.

Good leadership and an emphasis on employee welfare can improve a company's competitive position significantly. For example, in 1985 Jaynes Corporation, employing 200-250 people, faced escalating insurance and workers' compensation costs. So the company launched an intensive safety program, led by an unwavering commitment from top management. Through this program, the Safety Director reports directly to the Chairman and CEO, J. Howard Mock. Together with the supervisors and Executive Vice-President, they coordinate activities consistent with the corporate thrust, "Productivity Through Safety."

Jaynes has adopted a three-legged approach—an equilateral triangle comprised of safety, productivity and quality. Employees begin with a focus on safety; once they master these concepts, they concentrate on quality and productivity. Emphasizing the need for safety throughout the entire process, Jaynes requires the same safety procedures of their subcontractors and suppliers. A safety manager reviews each project regularly and prepares a report for the Project Supervisor, the CEO, and the Executive Vice-President of Field Operations.

Once top management agreed to the need and devised a preliminary plan, other layers of management became involved, from superintendents to crew foremen. To accomplish employee buy-in, Jaynes developed several programs. For example, they formed an Employee Relations Committee, where elected representatives from each craft in the field attend confidential meetings to convey their interests and safety concerns. Another program, Ideas Deserve Employee Awards (IDEA), rewards people for their ideas for procedural improvements.

Management's commitment to safety has brought extraordinary results. As a company, Jaynes Corporation ranked second in the nation in 1990 in the Large Contractor category, having worked 350,000 man-hours with no lost time or injuries. And in 1991, the company won the U.S. Senate Productivity Award and reduced its Workers' Compensation experience modifier by half. Further, quality and productivity have actually increased, during difficult economic times. While introducing this program, Jaynes's overall competitive market reduced to 40 percent. Yet within this period, the company actually grew—from $30 million to $70 million.

Usually customer requirements serve as the catalyst for implementing TQM, but not always. For instance, at Wal-Mart, a vendor partner sparked the interest by inviting Wal-Mart's top management to observe its quality process. A group of Wal-Mart executives, including Sam Walton, went to the vendor's home office and spent two days learning about their process.

After returning home, the executives agreed that although this approach worked well for manufacturing, they weren't convinced it would apply to a service-oriented business. Further, they concluded that many of the major concepts—such as sharing information with the associates and relying on them to make decisions—had been operating at Wal-Mart for a long time. But this vendor planted the TQM seed, and gradually, interest in TQM re-emerged within the organization.

Key Executive Training

Training, Step 2, is where a large fraction, preferably the entire Key Executive staff, undergoes initial TQM training. It can occur either off-site, or on the organization's premises. I prefer off-site training with all Key Executives in attendance. When all Key Executives are trained together, they can better understand the benefits of TQM to their organization with the advantage of interaction among them.

During this training, several important things occur. First, Key Executives begin aligning their thinking with the philosophy of TQM. For some, these concepts may be new, and their application not readily apparent. For this reason, a professional facilitator should encourage a high level of interaction. It is important to overcome the fear of change and address individual resistance to this new way of doing business. Because these issues will surface later with your subordinates, you must be prepared to deal with them.

It is also important to define and refine the terminology the company will use to communicate the quality process. As described earlier, in health care it is referred to as Continuous Quality Improvement (CQI); Summit Electric Supply Company refers to it as Total Quality Process (TQP); Xerox Business Products and Systems (Recipient of the 1989 Malcolm Baldrige Award) calls it "Leadership Through Quality"; at Fox Community College it's called, "Quality First"; and the U.S. Army calls it "Total Army Quality (TAQ)." During a recent conversation with a friend who works for an organization in Houston, Texas, I learned they call it TQLS—"Total Quality Lip Service." Apparently, everyone isn't on board yet.

What you call it may not be as important as selecting and agreeing upon terminology you can relate to. Many fumble in this one area. They use several sources of training for TQM, fail to coordinate terminology, and hence confuse people with a lot of different terms. This becomes an important point as the downward deployment of TQM begins throughout an organization. Everyone must be reading off the same sheet of music.

Assess Need for Consultant

Step three of Phase 0 addresses a widely debated topic in the Total Quality arena . Do I need to hire a consultant? The answer to this question depends on a number of factors including an organization's size, intrinsic talent, culture, and tempo, to name a few.

Larger organizations frequently hire consultants to design and debug a process before a major "roll-out," due to basic economics. If it takes one to two years to deploy a major new initiative throughout an organization, it's important to "get it right the first time." Changes in direction and focus confuse management and the workforce and arm personnel with sufficient ammunition to forestall the program.

If you have a cadre of internal consultants and trainers who feel comfortable at the front of the room and see TQM as a logical extension of their regular duties, you can save a lot of money. The challenge for these internal people is to create the focus and discipline to proceed on a given course. A consultant can accomplish this by charging exorbitant rates. And when word gets around that "the consultant" will be on site on the first of each month, people within the organization scurry to meet these milestones. I personally have consulted for organizations ranging from 10 to 30,000 people. I usually call at the half-way point between visits to discover what the client hasn't done in preparation for our next visit together. This simple reminder lights a fire to complete the agreed-to action items, so we can stay on track and get the most from our next visit. With very few exceptions, it is nearly impossible for an insider within an organization to create this discipline.

The exceptional cases I eluded to above stem from an organization's culture. If the prevailing attitude is one of "get the job done," or "we can do it," and Key Executives are used to creating a certain tempo and focusing on other major corporate initiatives, they may be able to implement TQM—assuming the correct skills base is brought to bear. Otherwise, plan on hiring a consultant. In most instances they are a bargain.

When first working as a consultant in 1977, I thought consultants were hired for their extensive specialty in a certain area. Although important, it is not the primary reason for hiring consultants. Other reasons include the need for specialized talent for a short period of time to expand the client's workforce. Frequently outsiders are brought into an organization to ask the difficult questions that would be awkward for insiders, and to infuse an experience element into the planning process to avoid "re-inventing the wheel." Such is the case with implementing TQM.

As a consultant, I can assure you that consultants recommend consultants much the same way physicians recommend other physicians. Professional ethics, honesty, and courtesy dictate recommending specialists where nothing less than the best will do. Since your credibility as an executive is at stake, you will want to seek the best.

Consultants are specialists. The benefits from the application of their expertise to a specific situation far exceed the cost. Their credibility and direct "hands-on" experience provide a faster and smoother transition toward Total Quality. Consultants have encountered and overcome the barriers and pitfalls of implementation; they possess detailed knowledge to minimize problems. For these reasons and many more, corporations routinely hire consultants.

Beyond training and advisement, outside consultants provide one other essential element for in-house trainers and facilitators—empathy. One of the best examples I've heard of empathy came up during a recent conversation with Rod Stewart, a retired Navy captain who is now a professional speaker on the subject of change.

As we swapped war stories, Rod spoke of the rescue of naval aviators during the Korean and Vietnam Wars. Before the 1950s, we rescued downed aviators from the decks of ships or with a whale boat, by coming along side and throwing out a life ring to them. Unfortunately, the time lapse between the mishap and the arrival of the ship was often so long that we lost many aviators.

The advent of the helicopter in naval aviation improved these rescue efforts. A helicopter could take off from an aircraft carrier, destroyer, or cruiser and reach the victim in a fraction of the time. The helicopter crew lowered a kapok ring, and the aviator raised his arms through the harness and held on to the noose in front of him. A winch on the helicopter hoisted him aboard, and then it was back to the ship for a spot of brandy.

This worked well, except for pilots incapable of participating in their own rescue; some suffered from hypothermia in the cold water, and others were physically injured. A man with a broken collarbone or a dislocated shoulder couldn't maneuver himself through the noose unassisted. With a sense of desperation, the helicopter crew sometimes watched helplessly as the aviators slipped beneath the surface of the sea.

The frustration over losing these near rescues drove the Navy to innovate. They put swimmers in wet suits on-board the helicopter. Now when they reached an aviator who was in bad shape, a swimmer immediately jumped into the sea, helped him into the noose, and followed him up to safety.

Interestingly, aviators who have been rescued in this manner often share a common sentiment. There was something magic in having a fellow sailor right there in the sea with them—enduring the same chilling water, the same threat of sharks, the same salt spray from the rotor wash from the helicopter—which gave them the strength and the courage to continue their difficult struggle.

Much like the downed aviators, internal trainers appreciate having someone nearby, sharing the perils of sharks. They, too, can maintain the resolve and the determination to complete a difficult task under less-than-perfect conditions.

Select Consultant

Only a few years ago a "TQM Consultant" was an anomaly, something special, and difficult to find. This has changed. Today you can find a moonlighting instructor from a local community college to share his speciality for probably fifteen to fifty dollars per hour, or an internationally recognized leader at twenty-five thousand dollars a day. (My rates are somewhere in between.) I hear you can find a TQM consultant next to every Taco Bell in Los Angeles—they're all over.

Also, a few years ago, many clients sought consultants to provide extensive introductory training on TQM. This is no longer the case. Today we see many companies (and individuals) doing extensive preliminary research on their own. Furthermore, when they do hire someone, they seek a well-defined specialist or generalist. Allow me to explain.

Companies planning to implement TQM, or larger companies dealing with specific problems, hire specialists to fill a specific need, a niche. Smaller companies seek generalists who can do everything from developing a strategic plan and facilitating team sessions, to conducting customer surveys, and so forth. They cannot afford the cost of the specialist, nor can they afford to bring in a steady flow of consultants to come up to speed on the details of their operation.

So a consultant, whether a specialist or a generalist, should be able to assist in forming expectations of results. A popular consultant response to the question, "When should I see results?" is, "It depends!" As it turns out, they're right. It does depend on many things. But, after spending time within the company, consultants should be able to suggest what kinds of results you should expect to see and when.

I emphasize this point specifically because management does have expectations, and without a satisfactory answer from the consultant, they will maintain their own expectations as the standard. If it takes too long, or if the magnitude of the first success is inconsistent with their expectations, bad things can happen. Typically, these "bad things" take the form of a breakdown in confidence between the corporate executive and the consultant. Worse yet, they can result in a changeover from one consultant to another. In that case, everyone loses.

Corporate executives should realize that changing consultants part way into the TQM implementation process is a big decision, resulting in a substantial cost in both time and money for the corporation. More important, this action will be viewed as a discontinuity by the workforce and managers looking for a reason to circumvent the initiative. If executives lose credibility in this area, the costs can be immeasurable.

During discussions with prospective clients, the subject of how long TQM implementation will take surfaces early. I try to be as honest as possible, explaining that they can reasonably expect some visible results within six to nine months from the decision to implement. That decision is made at the conclusion of Phase 1, Planning.

Having committed myself, I feel obligated to provide the following caveats: (1) the results from the first few PATs should provide needed process improvements without the expectation of earthshaking savings. The first few gestures toward process improvement should be guaranteed successes, selected to give PAT members experience in using the basic principles and tools of TQM and boost their self-confidence, and (2) these early results are merely the tip of the iceberg—a vote of confidence from corporate executives to convey their resolve for the initiative. The transition of the corporate culture, that point where process improvement becomes a way of life, takes by some estimate seven to ten years. This is a long-term commitment.

Now let me qualify that remark, because I'm putting myself on the line. I can think of one example where it took more than a year to derive direct benefit from the initial training investment; the organization had not done its homework. A TQM guru was hired to begin mass training before the organization executives even understood the importance of a cohesive set of terminology. In addition, the consultant had not been previewed by a representative from either the Corporate Council or Training Department, so he could not offer the audience hard-hitting, relevant examples of how TQM could benefit them. It took the organization more than a year to recover from that catastrophe and get back on track. And unfortunately, the executives realized a significant setback and loss of credibility in the process.

So where do the six to nine months come from? Assuming Phase 0 is complete (a decision to proceed with implementation has been made), it will take several months to accomplish initial corporate planning. Once begun, in-house support personnel are recruited and trained, teams are formed, and in approximately five months tangible results from their efforts should become evident. Six to nine months is ambitious, but achievable under the right circumstances. We'll discuss this topic and its underlying assumptions as we proceed through the book.

Corporate Strategic Planning

I have read enough on this subject to become thoroughly confused. So let me explain my perception of a corporate strategic plan and draw the connection between it and TQM.

Every company must have a purpose, a reason to be in business. I call it the Corporate Mission. Routinely, when thinking about the future of your company, you may draw a picture of a company that doesn't exactly coincide with its present product, service, or position within the industry. That's OK! That's your Corporate Vision—a statement of where you want to be in the future. It is that vital link between your mission and vision that forms the strategic plan, the road map that guides you to that new company, which presently exists only in your mind.

Exhibit 5-2 shows the division of responsibilities and elements necessary to put a corporate strategic plan in place. It all begins with the CEO defining the Corporate Vision. This vision translates into a set of Corporate Goals. Some goals, such as "Penetrate New Market," are long-term and may take five to ten years to occur. Others, such as "Reduce Customer Complaints," may be short-term, with visible signs of results being sought almost immediately. Corporate objectives express what or when a goal is accomplished. If a goal is to develop your human resources, an objective may be to allocate four percent of employee work hours to training over the next fiscal year. Objectives translate into the tasks, and eventually measurable parameters that are gathered by management and workforce personnel.

The downward deployment of this information conveys what is important to employees at all levels within the organization. Follow-up actions and their results can then be communicated back up through the corporate

94

hierarchy. After comparing the expectations to the actual results obtained, the company can make the necessary adjustments to keep on course. This important element of feedback, communication among different levels within the company, maintains a constant alignment between the highest and lowest levels in the organization. As you will see, the CEO uses the Corporate Vision to communicate to all employees what is valued, what is important, and where the company is going.

You've removed most of the road-blocks to success when you've learnt the difference between motion and direction.

Bill Copeland

EXHIBIT 5-2
Division of Responsibilities

Develop Vision Statement

Development of the organization vision statement is the first positive step toward TQM. Ideally, this takes place during a brainstorming session, typically off-site, with the aid of a trained professional facilitator. Here, via consensus, Key Executives arrive at a brief, concise statement as to why they are in business. It is normally expressed in terms of a commitment to quality, responsiveness to customer requirements, and a desire to become more competitive. Exhibit 5-3 provides some examples.

Development of the corporate vision statement always seems to give executives great difficulty. I like to use the following technique to meet the challenge. (1) Have each Key Executive brainstorm one ingredient, one term that is important for the vision statement and without which a major, important point would be lost. (2) Have the group arrive at a prioritized list of things that should be embodied in the vision statement. (3) Use that list to produce an outline of the vision statement and have the group develop several versions of how it should read. (4) Allow everyone to eventually arrive at a final product through iteration, consensus and review through the organization. I have shown some important terms in the examples listed in Exhibit 5-3. These include:

> *"provide products that conform to our customers' requirements,"*
>
> *"do the job right the first time," and*
>
> *"deliver error-free competitive products on time."*

My favorite is "we work together." I like it because it emphasizes the team aspect of our definition of TQM. "We work together!"

The vision statement must be easy to understand so everyone in the organization can relate to its meaning and his/her role in its success. I cannot overemphasize the importance of brevity. The "Lord's Prayer" contains 56 words, "Lincoln's Gettysburg Address" 268, yet the "Federal Government Regulation on the Sale of Cabbage" 26,911. Enough said.

EXHIBIT 5-3

Examples of Organization and Mission/Vision Statements

Vision Statement

"Bergen Brunswig Corporation will be the *Premier Provider* of Products and Services in all *Chosen Markets* and *Industries*, Acknowledged as a Leader in *Quality* and *Innovation*."

"We will be *Trusted* and *Respected* by our *Customers, Associates, Suppliers, Shareowners*, and *Communities* for the *Proven Commitment* to our *Mutual Success*."

Bergen Brunswig Corporation
Major Drug Wholesaler

Mission Statement

Increased member and staff satisfaction with pediatric department waits.

Relation to VISION:

- ❑ We are compassionate and caring, devoted to the health and well being of our members.
- ❑ We value our employees and the contribution of each.
- ❑ We provide leadership to the health care industry and serve as a model for the efficient delivery of quality health care.
- ❑ We foster innovation by valuing ideas.

Kaiser Permanente
Medical Care Program
Southern California Region

Mission Statement

The overall mission of the U.S. Geological Survey's Water Resource Division is to provide the hydrologic information and understanding needed for the best use and management of the Nation's water resources.

Vision Statement

To accomplish our mission, we recognize people as our greatest asset. Together we are dedicated to providing timely, high-quality hydrologic information and understanding to those we serve. To do this most effectively and efficiently, we have a responsibility to ourselves and each other to treat co-workers and other customers in a professional, courteous, and cooperative manner. As employees of a government agency, we will represent excellence to ourselves, cooperators, and the public.

The Employees of the New Mexico District
US Geological Survey

Vision Statement

We should share the vision of long-term profitable growth that will continue to position us as a premier supplier of professional services for capital facilities and technical systems.

- ❏ We are dedicated to customer satisfaction
- ❏ We are respected by customers and competitors alike
- ❏ We will strive to continue to be a company where people want to work and grow as talented and dedicated employees.

Sverdrup Corporation
St. Louis, MO

Vision Statement

An Organization Engaged in Relentless Customer-Driven Continuous Improvement

- ❏ Market Champion in Customer Satisfaction
- ❏ Market Champion in Delivering New, Value-Added Products and Services to Customers

iolab
a Johnson & Johnson Company

Vision Statement

We are the Aeronautical Systems Division, the center of excellence for research, development and acquisition of systems. We work together to create quality systems for combat capability to ensure we remain the best Air Force in the world and preserve the American way of life forever.

United States Aeronautical Systems Division
Wright-Patterson AFB, Ohio

Vision Statement

We will deliver defect-free competitive products and services on time to our customers.

IBM
Research Triangle Park, Raleigh

Vision Statement

Milliken and Company is dedicated to providing products and services designed to be at a level of quality which will best help its customers grow and prosper. Its operational area (Research and Development, Marketing, Manufacturing, Administration, Services) will be expected to perform its functions exactly as written in carefully prepared specifications.

Milliken Industries

Develop Corporate Goals

The corporate goals must flow from the organization vision statement described earlier. There may be many goals but, again, they must be concise. Exhibit 5-4 provides an example of an organization's corporate goals. From this sample, you see that the focus of this organization's corporate goals touches every aspect of the organization—from retaining technical excel-

EXHIBIT 5-4
Corporate Goals

Goal 0	Implement TQM
Goal 1	Retain Technical Excellence & Improve Quality
Goal 2	Increase Productivity of Direct Labor Force
Goal 3	Improve Financial Management
Goal 4	Reduce Cost of Material & Material Support
Goal 5	Maintain Capital Plant
Goal 6	Reduce Overhead Costs

Corporate Vision Statement — And Others

lence in its people, to maintaining a safe work environment.

I included Goal 0, "Implement TQM," to stimulate your thinking. It seems almost automatic for corporate executives to place this on their list of corporate goals. I mention this because I believe goals should be fluid, dynamic, changing with time. The corporate executive who places "Implement TQM" on this list may later discover that it needs to remain there forever. If removed, it can be construed that TQM is done, accomplished, finished. And as we all know, real TQM is a continuous process that goes on forever. So be aware of the perceptions you create in the minds of your people. The strategic plans, objectives, tasks and measurements will continue later in the process.

Outline Corporate Policy

Step 8 involves outlining corporate policy concerning TQM. A successful description of policy accurately conveys the corporate leaders' resolve to see TQM succeed. Key Executives will form the "skeleton" of policy. The "body" develops in Phase 1 through the Corporate Council. Here, the traditional system of rewards and recognition changes dramatically. Typically, subordinates are rewarded for accomplishments. The definition of accomplishment may expand to include attempts to apply a TQM principle or use a TQM tool that fell short of the expectations. This presents an opportunity to recognize people's best efforts, emphasizing that something less than "success" may be a step in the right direction.

Not all rewards have to be financial, and financial rewards don't have to be large. For example, Quadri Electronics Corporation, a leading manufacturer of military specification (MIL-SPEC) and radiation-hardened custom power supplies and memory systems, developed a reward system, called Quadri Bucks, to promote positive reinforcement among the 120 employees. Through this system, managers can provide personnel with instantaneous feedback and recognition—whenever they catch someone doing something right.

Typically, managers carry Quadri Bucks in their pockets and award them whenever they want to encourage a particular behavior. For instance, if a manager walking through the plant observes an employee stopping to pick up some trash on the ground, he or she could immediately fill out a Quadri Buck and hand it to that person. Employees can redeem them through the receptionist. She gives the employee four quarters, marks the Quadri Buck as paid, and returns it to the individual. Employees take pride in earning these Bucks; many display their stacks in a prominent place at their workstations.

Although any member of management can award Quadri Bucks to any non-management employee, they are often awarded by a member of the Quality Assurance Department to an assembly group producing a perfect board. Quadri Bucks have increased employee morale, but even more surprisingly, they have substantially improved production. Historically, one production area had been unable to produce zero-defect products the first time through. Yet within eight months of initiating the Quadri Bucks system, that same area produced more than 50 percent of the boards perfectly the first time. Further, the average production time for a board or board assembly decreased by one-third. When awarding Quadri Bucks for a perfect printed circuit board assembly, the management member announces the success in that person's work area, so the employees receive public recognition among their peers.

Despite the cash reward, this system isn't costing the company a lot of money. In fact, almost 40 percent of the Quadri Bucks are never redeemed. People are more interested in earning the Buck than receiving the money. Because this system has proven so successful, the Quality Assurance Department has asked the employees for ideas on ways to expand the concept. Suggestions they've received so far include providing special recognition for the top Quadri-Buck earners at a company picnic, or awarding a certificate of accomplishment to the top individuals at the end of each year. This employee input has confirmed one important fact in examining the success of the Quadri Bucks system. It's not the monetary value that keeps employees enthusiastic; it's the company-wide recognition. The trick is to choose the right form of recognition.

During a summer trip to the West Coast, I visited the *Queen Mary* on display in Long Beach, California. As we admired the ship's first-class dining room our guide told us a story. In the heyday of the *Queen Mary,* only actors, dignitaries, and the very wealthy could afford first-class accommodations. And within this prestigious group it was considered a great honor to be selected for seating at the captain's table. On one particular occasion, there were not enough celebrities and dignitaries to fill the table, so the captain decided to invite whomever had booked the most expensive suite. This passenger happened to be a Welsh coal miner, fulfilling a life-long dream of traveling in style aboard the ship. When the captain's steward knocked at the miner's door to deliver the gilt-edged invitation, the man was furious. "I've been saving all of my life to travel aboard the *Queen Mary,*" he said, "and now you want me to eat with the crew?" So when designing reward and recognition systems for promoting participation in the TQM process, we must be sure we're offering the right incentives to the right people.

Other policy issues that require attention include job security and management support. Job security is crucial today, as more and more companies downsize. This poses a genuine threat to everyone in the organization. For this reason, workers need assurance that they will not lose their jobs as a result of a productivity gain realized through TQM. Instead, personnel will begin working on other compelling needs within the company. This point must remain separate and distinct from the company's need to trim expenses due to economic downturns. This is a tough issue.

ITT Cannon Electric of Phoenix, Arizona for example, published its policy statements on quality in the policy and procedure manual. Combined, the elements to this policy set the tone with the following statement:

> ***"Overall Quality Policy"***
>
> ***Perform exactly like the requirement . . . or cause the requirement to be officially changed to what we and our customers really need."***
>
> ITT Cannon Electric
Phoenix Division

Management can convey support best by giving subordinates an opportunity to be heard at the top. A review entity must be formed to prioritize suggestions for consideration by the Corporate Council. The perceived fairness of this group determines whether or not people four levels into the organization really feel they have a pipeline to the top. This represents the executive link between management and the workforce.

Corporate Communication

It appears to have begun with Lee Iacocca, then Victor Kiam. Today it seems almost commonplace for corporate leaders, Presidents and CEOs to be highly visible in promoting their cause. Lee Iacocca sold America on the "New Chrysler Corporation." Victor Kiam liked the Remington company so much he bought it. Today's executives recognize that if they want their message heard, they better be the ones doing the talking.

> ***To be persuasive, we must be believable.***
> ***To be believable, we must be credible.***
> ***To be credible, we must be truthful.***
>
> Edward R. Murrow

To effectively communicate this message you must (1) know what the message is, (2) believe it yourself, and (3) deliver it yourself. All three things can be difficult for the corporate executive.

At the top of the list, you must know what the message is. If you have successfully arrived at this point in the TQM implementation process with a corporate vision statement you believe in, you are well on your way. You can transform it into a brief presentation you initially offer as a "canned speech." Later, as you refine your presentation, the script goes away and you will speak from the heart. I have included a speech I like as an example in Exhibit 5-5. Of course I like it—I wrote it.

EXHIBIT 5-5
Example Corporate Speech

I feel that each one of us at Technical Management Consortium,Inc. (TMC) must promise QUALITY to our clients. This is a commitment of on-going value by TMC. We pledge to provide error-free, interested and knowledgeable service to each client throughout the service life cycle. This pledge applies to each and every employee. This long-term vision and on-going quest for QUALITY sets us apart from competitors with short-term goals. In these days of mediocre service and lack of attention to detail, it is paramount for all of us to make this pledge and commitment to remind us of what our clients expect when they come to TMC.

Joseph R. Jablonski
President
March 1989

Points number two and three—belief and delivery—are frequently overlooked. Before becoming an independent trainer and consultant, I worked for the government for six years. There, I learned the value of having the people at the top convey support for an initiative by promoting it themselves. Mistakes I have frequently seen include delegating the communication responsibility to a subordinate, or using a routine communication mechanism to disseminate an important message. Often, routine communication from the top is accomplished via memos. If the CEO uses that same mechanism to convey the importance of TQM, the impact diminishes. Let me give you an example. Let's say the CEO describes his or her new thrust, a major initiative of great importance, by memo through the "chain of command."

Unbeknownst to the CEO, personnel receive memos at such a frequency that their level of importance has waned. The employee places the memo in a convenient location, along with all of the other "important" messages received over the past few months. Therefore, if TQM is really important to you, you must communicate the message by some means which sets it apart from all other messages. Nothing works quite as well as your personal presence.

> *Three things matter in a speech; who says it, how he says it, and what he says, and of the three, the last matters least.*

John Morley

Decision to Proceed

The tenth step in Phase 0 is a decision and a commitment of resources. Here, after completing the previous steps, the Key Executives elect to pursue implementation of TQM. This is done by committing resources to accomplish part of Phase 1, Planning. At this point, other executives in the company become acquainted with TQM. Involvement of the Key Executives is not over; they will soon make other decisions in Phase 1, concerning the expenditure of resources for full implementation.

The importance of the decision to commit resources cannot be overstated. This is a potential pitfall, where many fail if the CEO proceeds on to Phase 1 without making it absolutely clear that an important, far-reaching decision has been made. Some of the more popular techniques employed by CEOs to avoid making this important decision are (1) "I need more data" and (2) "I'll put someone else in charge." Both are potentially fatal.

"More data" is my favorite. This is where the CEO, unsure of his or her position, avoids the inevitable by merely asking for more and more data. This stall tactic results in dismal failure and a lack of credibility on future endeavors. The go-ahead to proceed into Phase 1 must be approached with enthusiasm—a religious fervor that TQM can truly benefit the organization. No degree of cost-benefit analysis, trade-off studies, or justification can sway disbelievers. Remember, if you had all the information you desired, you probably wouldn't need TQM. Decide. Make a decision, even if you choose to scrap the whole idea. That decision is better than no decision at all.

Putting someone else in charge is not an answer either. Corporate policy and direction cannot be delegated. When receiving TQM training, individuals in the audience always discuss who attended the session. They especially notice the presence or absence of the most senior people in the organization. That is not unreasonable. When Roland Peterson, President of Litton Industries, completed their 26-hour team training during a regularly scheduled class. His remarks after completing the class are inspiring.

> "I now understand from the inside how Perfect Teams work."

He goes on to say,

> "This will make it much easier for me to communicate the advantages of employee involvement to other divisions."

You, as a leader, must participate in the training process if you intend to convince subordinates of your resolve and communicate the importance of this valued initiative.

> *"Your expression is the most important thing you can wear."*
>
> Sid Ascher

Empowerment in the Quality Process

A popular term in America's quality movement today is empowerment. In any successful quality process everyone must understand what empowerment is, and even more importantly, how it applies.

Empowerment is a force that energizes people. Empowered personnel feel personal responsibility for contributing to the organization's success; they know they can directly influence how things get done. John Cleghorn, President of Royal Bank of Canada, was recently quoted in the *Toronto Globe & Mail* as saying, "quality companies put faith in their people...When employees see their opinions are valued, they see themselves making a difference to the success of the company. And they do." Empowerment, like TQM, is easy to describe, yet difficult to practice.

On the philosophical side of empowerment, management creates an atmosphere which maintains and enhances employee self-esteem. This includes establishing systems for employee suggestions to be voiced and acted upon. This does not mean that managers relinquish their power. As a matter of fact, they gain power by giving up power. It's far more effective to have 100 people pulling for your company vision, rather than a handful of executives pushing for it. Let's look at a couple of examples of empowerment.

In the 1970s G.E., Syracuse employed 17,000 people in the large-scale manufacturing of radios and televisions. Then, as the commercial electronics business moved out of Syracuse, the company concentrated on military electronics, gradually reducing the workforce to about 7,000 people by the mid '80s. In recent history, due to constrictions in the defense market and general downsizing, personnel has decreased to roughly 4,000. Today the primary product lines are commercial and military radar and sonar systems for both the U.S. and international markets; so to a large extent, the number and size of contracts won determines the optimum size of the workforce.

To combat a declining market and improve customer satisfaction, Jack Welch, the Chairman, has developed an employee empowerment program, called Workout. The program kicks off with town meetings, where 50 to 60 employees get together with a trained facilitator, who ensures reasonable participation from all the groups. Managers play a very low-key role; generally the senior executive helps start the meeting, explains the ideas to be discussed, and makes an exit. Then the participants break into groups of five or six people and talk about the things they really care about—like the quality of the cafeteria food or the parking problem. As they brainstorm ideas, enthusiasm swells, and everyone starts participating. Facilitators rotate among the groups, offering assistance where needed. Then the groups rank their ideas, gripes, or suggestions, in the order of priority and begin to brainstorm an action plan for implementing the improvements. After these teams develop a process action plan, top management returns to the room, and the groups present their ideas.

The town meeting generally takes 2 to 3 days. The first town meeting basically serves to clear the air and focus on the employees. Then, as employees become convinced they have the power to make decisions and change the status quo, the town meeting starts focusing on more business-oriented problems. G.E., Syracuse holds a town meeting every two months, in order to involve everybody.

Through this process, employees learn to identify a problem, select people who understand the process involved, choose a facilitator with no vested interest in the outcome, and have a Workout session to brainstorm possible solutions. After a Workout, the group makes recommendations to the appropriate management level. Workout teams can include external customers and suppliers, since they, too, can contribute ideas for process improvements. Since everyone in this organization knows that a focus on quality is the only real job security in the 1990s, they work to maintain their customers through quality products and services.

According to a former project manager of G.E., Syracuse, once a process like this has begun, there's no turning back. When the workers know that it's OK to ask questions and challenge the status quo, they will no longer accept the 1950s style of authoritative management. As he explained, "Once you've taught a bear how to dance, the bear decides when you'll stop dancing."

Chapter 6. Phase 1: Planning

Overview

During this phase the detailed implementation plan is developed, the supporting structure put in place, and the resources committed to accomplish implementation. Another important decision accompanies that of committing resources—determining the strategy for implementing TQM. Exhibit 6-1 summarizes the steps necessary to accomplish Phase 1, Planning. This phase requires the largest number of steps. The planning phase continues to develop the foundation upon which success stories will be derived later. In contrast to Phase 0, this phase does not end. Planning must be a continuous process since change never ceases in the external environment.

All companies need to plan, although for different reasons. A plan translates the cerebral into physical action. Have you ever initiated a change process in a company, only to have your people respond, "Gee that sounds good, but now what?" The plan answers the basic question, "Now what?" In some companies, the plan may account for consolidating office space and facilities in a new central location. In one case, a company wanted to implement TQM to improve its operation, leading to an improved company stock position, to yield a comfortable "nest-egg" for the CEO, who planned to retire in five years. So for many reasons, I must emphasize the corporate strategic plan as an integral part of any successful quality process. None of this happens in a benign environment.

"Adventure is the result of poor planning."

Author Unknown

EXHIBIT 6-1
Phase 1: Planning

△ **Form Team**
  △ **Council Training**
    △ **Identify Expectations for Results**
     △ **Identify Obstacles**
      △ **Select TQM Coordinator**
       △ **Train TQM Coordinator**
        △ **Strategic Planning (Continued)**
         △ Corporate Objectives
          △ Corporate Tasks
           △ Corporate Performance Measurements
            △ **Select Approach to Prioritize Process**
             △ **Select Processes for Improvement**
              △ **Bring Support Services on Board**
               △ **Develop Implementation Schedule**
                △ **Develop Implementation Budget**
                 △ **Decide to Proceed**

Step 1 of the Planning Phase involves propagating the spirit of TQM beyond the small cadre of Key Executives in Phase 0, to include all executive managers. Individuals now brought into the improvement process include all Corporate Council members. For the most part, members of the Council will be selected from the existing organizational chart. Not so for the TQM Coordinator. He or she will be hand-picked to serve as the "glue" that bonds together all aspects of this important initiative. The selection of this person should not be done in haste, as he or she will maintain a prominent position toward the top of the organizational chart commensurate with his or her responsibility.

I listened to the president of Maryland Bank speak on their quality initiatives during the October 1989 National Quality Forum. Impressed with his presentation, I decided to call his company and speak to the person in charge of quality. I was immediately transferred to their quality advocate, who proceeded to tell me about the advantages of their services, their turn-around time to replace stolen or missing credit cards, and the quality parameter they use to measure performance in the customer service department—the number of telephone rings before answering. She then tried to sell me on their MasterCard. I was impressed by the way they strive to satisfy the needs of their customers. As it turned out, she was a vice president. Not surprisingly, companies successful in Total Quality always manage to assign the appropriate rank structure with the position.

Forming the Team

To successfully implement TQM, the existing organizational hierarchy must be transformed into the team that will make TQM a reality. This renewed structure will become one of three elements included in Exhibit 6-2, the Corporate Council, Process Action Teams (PATs), and Support Services.

> *In the end, all business operations can be reduced to three words: people, products, and profits. People come first. Unless you've got a good team, you can't do much with the other two.* (Iacocca, 1984).

Lee Iacocca

EXHIBIT 6-2
Team Elements Necessary to Implement TQM

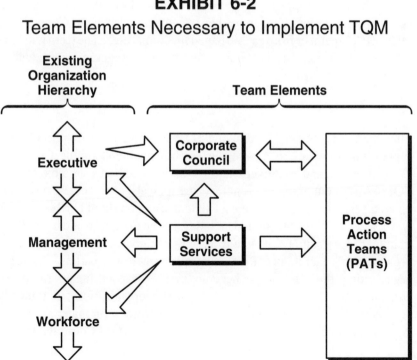

Corporate Council

The Corporate Council consists of a leader and the organization's functional managers. The leader is the CEO or President. Functional managers, the next layer below the CEO, may be Vice-Presidents, Directors, etc. Remember, the Council includes those individuals who actively participated in Phase 0. The Council now has the responsibility to implement policy, to develop and implement the TQM plan, and to create, empower and support PATs. The Council also reviews, analyzes, and improves processes within the organization with the aid of PATs and the advice of the TQM Coordinator. *The greatest responsibility of the Council is to remove barriers between functional entities within the organization and facilitate communication to show support and overcome the resistance PATs will inevitably encounter.* Council members are trained prior to creating the first PAT.

Process Action Teams

Process Action Teams are chartered by the Council once it has selected a process for improvement. Commonly, one member of the PAT will have suggested the idea being addressed. PATs can include a mixture of workforce, management, and executives; the Council selects the exact composition based upon the process under study. To facilitate communication for processes involving more than one functional area, the Council may select a PAT member from each affected functional area. The team will later select one PAT member, not necessarily the highest ranking individual, to serve as the team leader.

Support Services

This, the third element, is led by the TQM Coordinator, who provides the supporting resources to ensure the smooth operation of the Corporate Council, PATs, and employee training. Support Services should include a TQM library containing relevant texts, periodicals, case studies, audio and video tapes, training lessons, etc . Content selection should be based upon two considerations. (1) It should include relevant material to aid in the TQM training process, and (2) it should serve as a ready resource to support the organization's facilitators, PATs, and other interested parties. In larger organizations the TQM library becomes part of the assets in the Training or Human Resources Departments. In smaller organizations, it typically occupies a shelf or two plus a file cabinet drawer of materials in the Administration Department or in the office of the TQM Coordinator.

Council Training

In Step 2, Training, remaining Council members will be trained, along with the TQM Coordinator, if he or she is selected by this time. As in Phase 0, this training includes an introduction to the principles, concepts, and tools of TQM. To insure a broad-based understanding of management issues, the TQM Coordinator should receive supplemental training on TQM tools and facilitation skills. This knowledge will prove useful because the full-time TQM Coordinator will facilitate meetings regularly, advise all levels within the organization, and match consulting support with the specific needs of Process Action Teams.

In some instances, depending on how extensively the key executives have researched the quality process, this training session can yield the implementation plan itself. Over the span of about three days, the Corporate Council can receive initial training and develop the list of items already accomplished, which brings them closer to implementation. A list of "2-Be-Done" items (refer to Exhibit 4-3) eventually becomes their implementation schedule milestones.

First Corporate Council Meeting

Once the Corporate Council members and the TQM Coordinator have been selected and trained, they can proceed to their first TQM Council Meeting. Several specific items should be discussed during the first Corporate Council meeting: the Council's charter, division of responsibilities necessary to support the implementation plan, and an upcoming schedule of events, to name only a few. The Council also has hands-on involvement in preparing the implementation plan. They approve it and are responsible for the inevitable "mid-course" adjustments that will be necessary as circumstances change. Exhibit 6-3 provides a sample agenda for this first meeting.

Although these meetings will occupy a substantial amount of time early on, the goal is to eventually meld these activities into ongoing business procedures, so they become part of your regular business practice. So how do you do this? By merging the Corporate Council's activities into regular monthly or bimonthly executive meetings.

EXHIBIT 6-3
Sample Agenda for First Corporate Meeting

- ❏ Call Meeting to Order
- ❏ Introduce Council Members
- ❏ Introduce TQM Coordinator
- ❏ Review Draft Charter
- ❏ Review Roles & Responsibilities of Council Members & TQM Coordinator
- ❏ Review Upcoming Schedule of Events

  Develop Expectations for Results

  Implementation Plan Draft Due

  Implementation Plan Approval

  Selection of Implementation Strategy

  Identification of Critical Processes & Objectives

  Support Services On Board

  Communication Prepared
- ❏ Define Division of Responsibilities to Prepare Implementation Plan
- ❏ Schedule Next Meeting
- ❏ Adjourn Meeting

Once we move past the planning activities, which occupy the greatest amount of time, the Council begins to work on forming, maintaining and approving PAT recommendations. It would not be uncommon for an executive-level PAT to address such corporate-wide processes as communications, relocating facilities, reorganization, etc.

Identify Expectations for Results

Early in the planning process we, as Corporate Council members, must develop our expectations. We must understand what we wish to obtain from this effort. I think Kevin Hull, an environmental manager, put it well when he said, "people are allergic to planning." Though tedious and time-consuming, planning is essential in the quality process. We must know our objectives—the decisions we need to make—before we begin. Otherwise, we have no way of gauging the quantity and quality of the data we need to collect. Thorough planning helps us eliminate the possibility of collecting wrong or excessive information and focus on the most efficient approach to the problem. The information we collect serves as feedback to corporate executives on how our goals contribute to increased customer satisfaction and higher profits. So in contrast to conventional wisdom, most American managers are mature in their thinking to recognize that "employee wellness" does yield an improved bottom line. By documenting these expectations early on, we have a measuring stick for assessing how the quality process is going six months, or a year or so into the future.

Identify Obstacles

People are consistent and predictable in this area. Resistant to change, they consciously or unconsciously present obstacles to any new initiative. TQM implementation is no different; people resist it...well, for a lot of reasons. Resistance to change is inevitable, even when change offers improvement. This resistance consists of a mixture of real and perceived difficulties, not only within the workforce, but in management and the executive level as well. Whether real or imagined, each resistance identified must be met head-on with positive, enthusiastic support. Management's ability to overcome resistance early helps eliminate much of the fear and anxiety associated with change.

The best defense is a good offense! Anticipate resistance and establish mechanisms to overcome it before it creates a major problem. One of the best vehicles to accomplish this is awareness and orientation training for employees. You can also alleviate resistance through the organization's policy statement. If tied directly to employee recognition and rewards, the policy statement(s) will convey a positive message to both management and workforce. When developed properly and stated correctly, it can have workers saying to themselves, "Yes, I can also benefit from TQM by taking a chance." If employees become convinced they will gain something, you're on the right track. Employee benefits may include better working conditions, less frustration within the corporate structure, and possibly, financial reward.

The Corporate Council can contribute significantly to implementing TQM. Again, if done correctly, their mere presence conveys a message to the workforce: "We're with you 100%." Here, the Council can pat someone on

114

the back for merely suggesting a good idea. Further support is displayed by committing the corporate resources to charter new PATs. Last and most important, the Council removes barriers that make straight-forward solutions so difficult. The PAT members will have their hands full understanding, analyzing, and developing recommendations for the Council. In return, the Council must overcome the political umbrella which surrounds the problem being addressed by the PAT, across functional divisions of responsibility.

Some potential problems for Council consideration are included in Exhibit 6-4. Suggested solutions and approaches to resolving them are also provided. Executives may memorize these solutions or develop new ones, using their own "English" or personal beliefs. You will hear or see these again in real life.

Select TQM Coordinator

As mentioned earlier, the Corporate Council members are typically pulled from the organizational chart and represent the top two layers of management, which I call executives. Not so for the TQM Coordinator. This person is hand-selected to fill this important role. Some guidance on the traits or characteristics you may find desirable in this person is included in Exhibit 6-5. In fact, this criteria applies for anyone you may be considering for a TQM Facilitator position as well.

A brief review of Exhibit 6-5 can be intimidating, so let me put you somewhat at ease by stating that these people don't really exist. And if they did, you probably couldn't afford to hire them. But some of these attributes are essential.

For example, Number 3 is important; you want someone with a track record of successfully introducing innovation and achieving organizational commitment. Number 5 is imperative—the TQM Coordinator must possess good interpersonal and communication skills. Remember, this person will attend all Corporate Council meetings and frequently give presentations both within and outside the organization. You also want someone who will be around long enough so you can capitalize on this investment (Number 10). While I could easily elaborate on all ten criteria, I will close by emphasizing one more especially important factor. You need a volunteer, someone who really wants to do this (Number 6).

EXHIBIT 6-4

Compilation of Some Likely Resistance-to-Change Issues and How They Might Be Overcome

Potential/Probable Issues	Suggested Solution or Approach
Management doesn't care.	We now realize the importance and value of our employees. Through TQM we wish to bring the workforce into the corporate decision-making process on issues affecting their careers and their jobs. Participative management is a basic part of TQM's definition.
I don't believe TQM can work in our company.	The principles and tools of TQM have been successfully applied throughout thousands of service and manufacturing organizations. Our goal is to learn the basics of TQM so we can begin creating success stories within our own company.
We do not have the resources to support this initiative.	Yes, the implementation of TQM will cause all of us to sacrifice precious time. We will all be doing double duty, but this investment will yield great dividends. This initiative will actually save us time and money in the long term and will make us more competitive.
There is no continuity of leadership to support this initiative.	Yes, turnover at all levels is always a problem. If we demonstrate success early on, and establish ourselves as being on track, no future staff will argue with our proven success, and we can continue the TQM process of improvement.

EXHIBIT 6-5
TQM Coordinator/Facilitator Selection Criteria

1. A mix of personnel from different levels within the organization.
2. People who have credibility.
3. People with a track record of successfully introducing innovation and achieving organizational commitment.
4. People who are known to be team players and have the leadership capacity to bring together the thinking of the group.
5. People with good interpersonal and communication skills.
6. Volunteers! They must really want to do this.
7. People who have a strong personal belief in the participative ethic.
8. People who can constructively confront the status quo and still work effectively with those in positions of authority.
9. People who are self-secure and able to maintain clear thinking in conflict situations.
10. People who will be around for a while.

During a recent presentation, someone asked me an important question: "Does the TQM Coordinator really have to volunteer for this job?" I responded by telling a story about a recent trip my son, Joey Jr., and I took to Camp Frank Rand, a Boy Scout camp in northern New Mexico. We checked in late on Friday afternoon, settled into our camping area, ate a snack, and went to bed. The next morning we attended the opening ceremony at the flag pole. Afterwards they asked all parents to report to the check-in area near the parking lot. When we arrived we were told, "Thank you for volunteering."

For the entire day, I taught 23 groups of elementary school children how to read a map, pace off distances and read a direction (bearing) on a compass. Let's make no mistake, I was *volunteered*. But like so many other parents who "were volunteered" I pitched in and did my part. We all contributed, and I believe that this active participation made the trip more enjoyable for all of us. If you do not have children in scouting, but have spent time in the military, this procedure may sound familiar to you. So to answer the question, "Does the TQM Coordinator need to volunteer?" More directly, the answer is a resounding yes—but some may need more encouragement than others.

Train TQM Coordinator

Once you have a TQM Coordinator, what do you do with this individual? You provide training. Exhibit 6-6 provides an example of the type of training TQM Coordinators should receive. These skills will prepare them to understand the complete scope of continuous process improvement in both the technical and non-technical skills areas. They will learn how to carry a PAT from beginning to end, from training and facilitation, to internal consulting and coaching.

EXHIBIT 6-6
TQM Coordinator/Facilitator Training

Lesson 1:	Introduction
Lesson 2:	Group Dynamics
Lesson 3:	Team Roles & Responsibilities
Lesson 4:	Communication Skills
Lesson 5:	Consensus
Lesson 6:	Ground Rules and Operating Procedures
Lesson 7:	Group Development/Individual Behaviors
Lesson 8:	Contracting
Lesson 9:	Active Interventions
Lesson 10:	Making Meetings Work
Lesson 11:	Introduction to Decision-Making Model
Lesson 12:	Brainstorming
Lesson 13:	Fishbone Diagram
Lesson 14:	Flow Charting
Lesson 15:	Statistical Studies
Lesson 16:	Interviews/Surveys
Lesson 17:	Cost of Poor Quality
Lesson 18:	Prioritization Methods
Lesson 19:	Graphs/Charts
Lesson 20:	Control Charts
Lesson 21:	Force-Field Analysis
Lesson 22:	Stakeholder Analysis
Lesson 23:	Cost/Benefit Analysis
Lesson 24:	Basic Statistics

Select Approach to Prioritize Processes

Next, the Council selects an implementation strategy. You may use one or more of four basic approaches in selecting problems for PATs:

1. The Top-Down Approach
2. Good Ideas from Employees
3. Customer Suggestions
4. Chronic Problems

The Top-Down approach provides a logical audit trail from the organization's vision statement, through goals, to objectives and the assignment of PATs, based upon a demonstrated relationship between problem resolution and corporate objectives. This is a good approach from an accounting perspective, but it can be difficult to get PAT support and personal commitment from the workforce. Because the ideas generally belong to someone else, this approach is more consistent with a management style that prevailed before TQM.

Sometimes benchmarking can help you decide which processes to select for improvement. And occasionally, benchmarking against your competitors is not enough, as in the case of Wal-Mart. From the very beginning, this company always learned from their competition. In fact, Mr. Sam encouraged all associates to visit their competition and insisted that they concentrate on even small things the competitor was doing that could improve Wal-Mart's operation.

To begin learning about the right approach for Wal-Mart to take in TQM, the competition didn't have visible results to benchmark against, so Wal-Mart knew that they had to go outside the retailing environment to learn about successful approaches. In 1990, the executives decided to ask a team of associates to investigate the TQM approaches of companies such as Proctor and Gamble, IBM, Hershey Chocolate, G.E., Xerox, Milliken Industries, and Dow Chemical. They sent strategic leaders who knew Wal-Mart well to examine these companies' approaches knowing that they would evaluate what they saw with a critical eye. The executives knew that the team would recommend only TQM approaches which would enhance the competitive position of the entire company.

After a four-month period, this team presented its findings to the Executive Committee. The executives were as surprised as the team has been to learn that other companies were doing a better job in some areas—and looked as those as opportunities for improvement for Wal-Mart. For example, they found that Hershey had a similar, people-oriented culture and that their people philosophies were more consistently executed because of deep commitment to nurturing and carrying on the legacy left by Milton S. Hershey. From G.E. they heard the power of the "three S's" that drive G.E.'s business: speed, simplicity and self-confidence. Everyone had to agree that these methods made good business sense for Wal-Mart, too. So when the competition fails to offer new insight, it pays to look beyond the obvious sources for new standards and ideas.

Option 2 is one of my favorites, supporting good ideas from the employees. Getting employees to "buy into" the improvement process is not an easy task. But, workforce resistance can be overcome, if the Council supports an employee's idea and provides the necessary resources to succeed. Everyone wins under this option.

For instance, when Computer One™ realized their kan-ban carts could not adequately handle the increase in all the warehouse activity, management faced a decision. They could either switch to larger carts to facilitate product flow, or they could buy more carts of the same size. After evaluating the situation and brainstorming with the associates, they determined that more carts of the same size would improve the process considerably, because they could load products and transport them through the processes more quickly, thus increasing output.

Whenever Computer One decides to improve a particular process, associates report back on the progress during their weekly Wednesday meetings. They look at the figures from the past week to see if cycle-time improved. As a result, they've managed to reduce inventory considerably. Additionally, associates have learned to correct their own mistakes, resolving more problems before they ever reach the company president. Consequently, the top management spends less time "putting out fires." This actually translates into one extra day off per week for the CEO—something we can all appreciate.

Option 3, a customer suggestion, should not be ignored. Mr. Joe Girard, "The Greatest Salesman in the World," according to *Guinness Book of World Records*, suggests that one dissatisfied customer has the ability to turn away up to 250 potential customers. Furthermore, most customers don't complain to you. They complain to their friends, and they just don't come back. For these reasons and more, you should make every effort to keep good customers by demonstrating immediate results in resolving their complaint. A complaining customer, despite conventional wisdom, is an asset and may surface opportunities for process improvement that your own people may have overlooked.

A customer complaint should prompt the company to investigate the source of that problem immediately. But you don't have to wait for negative feedback. An even better method of gaining input comes from carefully developed customer surveys. Computer One™ routinely solicits customer comments by including surveys in their newsletter, *Computer OneLink*. They design and mail these surveys selectively—sometimes focusing on the retail customer base, and at other times, gearing the surveys specifically to groups within one major customer's organization.

Finally, Option 4 is the Chronic Problem. This is a problem that has plagued your organization for as long as anyone can remember; it costs both money and time, creating frustration regularly. I suggest postponing these problems until professional help arrives, or until after you have experienced some successes in process improvement. It is unlikely that any individual within the organization will possess the necessary objectivity and skill to tackle such problems early in the implementation of TQM. This is where hired consultants can be put to good use. Moreover, attacking this type of problem early on can easily result in failure, which impedes progress toward TQM in the future.

A summary of the four problem-selection criteria, as well as some pros and cons of each, is included in Exhibit 6-7. Personal experience causes me to favor Options 2 and 3 above. I've found it preferable to support the ideas of the workforce and customers first. A simple explanation clarifies that statement. If you, as an organization leader or Council member, support your employees and customers early on, you will probably have sufficient time to tackle the bigger problems in the future. The reverse is not always true.

I will close with two pointers for easing the burden of selecting problems to be addressed by PATs: (1) Offer a clear path to success for the first few problems you address. After your people have been trained, a light may go off in their heads; you'll hear a snap of the fingers; and someone will say, "Wasn't that obvious?" These are easy candidates for TQM. (2) From the onset, PATs should be able to see the light at the end of the tunnel. There

EXHIBIT 6-7

Problem-Selection Criteria Options Available to the Corporate Council

Options	Pros	Cons
Top Down	Relates PAT assignments directly to Organization Vision Statement.	Risks overlooking compelling or more costly problems.
Good Idea from Employee	Supports and encourages more ideas from employees.	Employees offering the suggestion may feel overlooked if their idea is not selected.
Customer Suggestion	"The customer is always right."	Mechanism must be in place to provide feedback to organization.
Chronic Problem	Everyone recognizes this is a long-term problem which must be resolved.	May be too difficult to tackle in the early phases.

will be time to tackle the big problems later. In the beginning, look for quick turn-around time to gain feedback both from your successes, and from the things that did not go exactly as expected. To emphasize, initially select TQM projects which insure a clear path towards success and quick turn-around time.

Select Processes for Improvement

At this point, it is common to feel overwhelmed. So many processes thrive within an organization (hundreds, maybe thousands), that it seems difficult to select those first few processes for teams. Let me offer you one suggestion.

Recently I worked with a one-hundred person professional services firm that had the same dilemma. Their strategic plan surfaced top management interest in developing human resources. Employee feedback reflected the absence of a distinct career path for individual growth within the organization. Customer feedback suggested training deficiencies in field personnel. Though distinctly different observations, the common denominator in all three instances was training. And if you follow the approach described in this book, eventually lights will begin to flash on, and you will see a clear course of action. Trust me.

Bring Support Services on Board

This element includes the top TQM individual within the organization, the TQM Coordinator, as well as a mixture of consulting and training services. Organizationally, the TQM Coordinator resides at a level directly below the CEO in a staff role at parity with the deputy or a senior V.P. It is the full-time responsibility of the TQM Coordinator, with the aid of others in Support Services, to serve as arms, legs, and advisor to the Council. The TQM Coordinator plays a key role in developing and integrating the TQM Implementation Plan and aids in prioritizing suggestions for PATs based upon the Council's selected criteria. One responsibility is closely coordinating the training portion of the implementation plan with the company's training department. The TQM Coordinator also represents the organization in interface meetings involving other companies, divisions, sub-divisions, superior and subordinate organizations, as well as suppliers, on issues related to TQM. As a regular participant in Council meetings, he or she will also serve as its secretary.

Consulting services include a combination of in-house and hired consultants for routine and non-routine consulting assistance to the organization. Individuals within the organization who desire consulting services arrange these activities through the TQM Coordinator. It should be the eventual goal of the organization to have the large majority of this support accomplished by in-house people. Consulting services provide one-on-one aid to the TQM Coordinator, the Council, and middle managers needing specific assistance in resolving TQM issues. The majority of in-house consultant time will be spent helping the PATs better understand the use of specific TQM tools and applying them to specific goals. In some ways, consulting services become an extension of formal training to PAT members. Remember, it is the responsibility of the PATs—not the consultants—to do the work.

The final Support Service is training. Because of the dynamics of this responsibility, early training will probably be accomplished by some form of contracted services with in-house assistance. This is due to the changing expertise of the trainers. The early phases require a heavy emphasis on concepts and principles. Later, training will shift, focusing on management and technical aspects. PAT members may need specialized training in small numbers, tailored to their task.

Let us summarize a few of the important points covered above. First, it is the responsibility of the TQM Coordinator to insure that training requirements flow from the corporate strategic plan, through the implementation plan, and become relevant, scheduled training classes. The organization training department interviews, selects, budgets, and schedules training in close coordination with the TQM Coordinator.

Other Considerations in Planning

Before we move on to discussing the schedule and budget items associated with TQM implementation, a few important, though often unsavory, topics must be addressed. They are union involvement and corporate downsizing. Each can have a profound impact on your schedule, budget and achievement of the expectations you are reaching for.

For various reasons corporate management does not always look favorably on labor unions, although unions must become an integral part of any quality process. Union motives for participating in the quality process are often similar to those of management—survival. I recently did some work for a company in Ontario, Canada, where a significant portion of the blue-collar employees belonged to the Communications and Electrical Workers of Canada (CEWC). In a paper presented at their 7th Annual Convention in Quebec in May 1990, union leaders described their agenda for addressing employers' movement into Quality Circles, Team Concepts, Quality of Worklife, Multi-Skilling, and so forth. Verbiage such as, "We are not on the same team, but we have to recognize, in many ways, we share the same house," illustrates their basic unwillingness to participate as a "team-player," but also acknowledges some realities of life. The union prefers the term, "intelligent cooperation."

Management is responsible for making the infusion of a quality process into any organization as palatable as possible. The issue of union participation is not simple and straightforward. And you, as a corporate leader, must account for them in the planning process. I typically offer clients the following advice on this important topic: if you do involve union leadership early in the planning process for quality, it *may* eventually cause you problems. If you overlook this one point, it *will* cause you problems later on down the road.

The second topic that needs to be addressed during planning is downsizing. Some have gone so far as to rename it "right-sizing." Whatever the terminology, the bottom-line answer is the same; people will lose their jobs. I recently read an article in the local newspaper summarizing the results of a consultant's study. Seventy-five percent of the companies surveyed have undergone downsizing at least once during the past five years. The phenomenon, rampant in America, begs to be understood in its relationship to a TQM process.

If a company confronts the need to downsize with no TQM program in place, this probably isn't a good time to start a program. Because people's minds are elsewhere, it's hard to generate enthusiasm for a new concept. But if downsizing occurs in a company with an active TQM program, the tools of process improvement can add invaluable insights and improve the bottom line. We measure quality not only by the finished product, but also by the amount of effort required for producing that result. A quality focus— especially during downsizing—reduces unproductive activities. With fewer resources, we must focus on maximizing what we have.

One simple way to increase productivity is by trimming non-value-added steps from a process. For example, at one time G.E., Syracuse required one-over-one manager approval for overtime. If a department needed employees to work overtime, the manager's manager had to approve it. But because these managers trusted their subordinates' judgment, they always approved the overtime. Therefore, the second manager's approval served no real purpose. So the company stopped requiring that approval and eliminated one non-value-added step in the process.

Seemingly small process improvements like this can add up to a substantial savings of time and money. As the 1980s ended, this company confronted a grim reality—a cycle of financial losses for six consecutive years. The shrinking defense budget had eliminated major contracts, so the need for downsizing became apparent. But in 1990, following the introduction of a quality improvement program, the picture changed considerably. Despite all the downturns in its market, G.E., Syracuse turned a profit in 1991 and fully expects to do so again in 1992.

After a downsizing, TQM skills can assist overworked employees by streamlining work activities. So what is the relationship between a quality process and TQM implementation? Scheduling.

Develop Implementation Schedule and Budget

We are proceeding to the third major decision for the Corporate Council, "Decide to Proceed." To make an intelligent decision, the Council must understand the cost implication and have a reasonable schedule for seeing results in the quality process. These two basic elements comprise the plan for implementation. Earlier, the Council members formulated their expectations for results. These expectations, accompanied by the budgeting line items, belong on the schedule. Chapter 10 provides an in-depth look at the schedule, and Chapter 11 addresses the matter of budgeting.

Decide to Proceed

Approval of the implementation plan and a decision to proceed will transpire smoothly if everyone participates in its development, and there are no last-minute surprises. The difficulty comes in committing resources. The issue of money always seems to be a problem, but here it becomes an especially sensitive issue, due to the magnitude of the dollars involved. It may require a reallocation of budgets within the organization, or a request for support from a senior organization. Regardless of how this is accomplished, we must recognize this as a long-term investment, from which the organization can expect a substantial return.

Where Others Have Failed or Fumbled

So many books describe success and how to improve that we often forget that failures creep in along the way. Not all experiences are positive, but we can learn from them if they lead to intangible benefits for those involved. This section discusses where others have encountered difficulty in implementing TQM, so we might learn.

It is timely to review this important topic now, since we can relate directly to the five-phase implementation methodology above and avoid some common pitfalls. For review, the five phases in the TQM process are: (0) Preparation, (1) Planning, (2) Assessment, (3) Implementation, and (4) Diversification. Each phase has potential for problems if not handled correctly. Let us review some more common errors I have witnessed from observing the implementation of change.

Phase 0 - Preparation. The most common error Key Executives make here is the decision to proceed. Some believe you can actually make the wrong decision to implement a corporate-wide quality process. From my experience, failure only arises from making a half-decision, a half-hearted effort to implement TQM when you, yourself, are not thoroughly convinced of its benefits. Presidents or CEOs who delegate this important initiative to a subordinate have not understood the importance of top management commitment. They treat it like any other program where they are briefed on progress, cost, and schedule, without taking an active part in making it a reality. This is where many fail. If TQM, as a major corporate initiative, is neither approved nor disapproved, but rather put in place with perfunctory, half-steps, it cannot succeed. We observe striking examples of this point in government's efforts to move toward Total Quality. Regulations and directives motivate few, if any, people. Therefore, the challenge in government is to convince individual organizations of the need for change. In the private sector this is not too difficult. Either people produce, or the company folds. In government the difficulty is convincing people of the need for change and showing them how they will benefit by helping the change take place. That is a tough thing to do.

Phase 1, Planning, is another place where corporate executives can experience heartache. In this phase, the goal is to begin the downward deployment of TQM and involve all corporate executives. Failures sometimes occur from not providing enough time or incentive to convince all executives of the need for this change. All executives must accept this process and begin to appreciate the magnitude of the immanent change. If everyone involved in the planning phase does not perceive a meaningful gain in implementing TQM, fall back, regroup, and go through the drill again until the whole group agrees. As Lee Iacocca says, "Commitment to quality is like a commitment to religion. It pervades everything (by necessity)" (Iacocca, 1984).

The most spectacular failure I've seen in planning to implement TQM occurred at McDonnell Douglas Aerospace Corporation (DAC) in Long Beach, California. DAC is currently the third largest producer of commercial aircraft, in terms of gross revenue. The number one and two spots are held by Boeing and a European consortium of companies called Airbus. DAC called its initiative TQMS, Total Quality Management System. Its downfall, although attributed to many factors, came from ignoring the basic scheduling aspect I described earlier.

DAC's CEO got the company off to a poor start in February 1989. The cornerstone of this new initiative was teamwork, a focus pioneered by W. Edwards Deming. The teamwork concept serves to drive out fear and foster trust between workers and management. But DAC did the exact opposite, by telling its 5,200 middle managers and executives that they had lost their jobs and would have to compete for 1,000 fewer positions. Deming, himself, said from his Washington D.C. office, "It's a good way to produce chaos. It's the worst thing to do."

I had first heard of this "musical chairs" approach to downsizing in the summer of '89 at a Toastmasters International Convention in Palm Desert, California. During an evening function in a room filled with 1,400 fellow Toastmasters, I somehow managed to sit beside an engineer from DAC. As he described DAC's downsizing procedure to me and cited the close timing of the TQMS implementation, I simply couldn't believe it. (Later, DAC officials would be quoted as saying it was part of their overall TQMS strategy.) So don't overlook the basics when planning the roll-out of your TQM initiative. People are extremely sensitive to the perceived relationship of quality, productivity, and job loss.

Phase 2, Assessment. This phase requires a strong sense of self-security, asking your people for feedback on the strengths and weaknesses of the organization and comments on how they interpret your leadership at the management and workforce levels. The greatest challenge to the corporate executive here is committing the time and money to having a proper organizational assessment conducted. Though many aspects of the Assessment phase can be accomplished by in-house personnel, the organizational assessment most often cannot. This can become another pitfall for many companies; top management surveys personnel, asking difficult questions that are best handled by an independent person with no vested interest in the outcome. To avoid this potential pitfall, I suggest you seek and retain the best talent available to accomplish the organizational assessment. It is essential.

Phase 3, Implementation. A common problem occurs when mass training is begun for all management and workforce personnel before resolving some very basic issues. These issues, which may insure success or failure, result directly from what has happened in the three previous phases. Before group training begins in Phase 3, two things must have been accomplished:

(1) All executives must be in "sync" as to the need and importance of implementing TQM. Everyone, including the CEO, must be convinced that something valuable will be gained from making TQM happen.

(2) The results from the organizational assessment must be used in the planning process (Phase 1) to ascertain the training needs of the organization. While much of the initial TQM training is fairly standard, establishing terminology, pinpointing specific cases, and other factors must be considered in tailoring this information for management and workforce personnel. Then, and only then, will people leave a TQM training session with a positive feeling that the information they've heard applies to them.

Phase 4. Diversification. The most common problem I see here is one of timing. It is not uncommon for an organization to not do its homework (i.e. Planning, Assessment, and Implementation) and to "roll-out" a major quality initiative, immediately involving suppliers and subordinate organizations. Again, if you have not experienced the rewards (and challenges) of implementing a quality process yourself, it is difficult to communicate its merits to others. As we will see when we discuss Phase 4, Diversification in greater detail later, this can spell failure for TQM and other corporate initiatives and detract from your credibility.

These pitfalls do not necessarily dictate failure, but they can short-circuit your best intentions and postpone the realization of that first success story by six months, a year, or more. If these remarks are taken as intended, you will be safe in the knowledge you did not reinvent some of the failures experienced by others.

Chapter 7. Phase 2: Assessment

Phase 2, Assessment, includes six steps as outlined in Exhibit 7-1, from quick-assessment through training feedback. These assessment tools establish internal and external channels of communication throughout the organization, providing a continuous flow of information to the Council for planning purposes. Once obtained and analyzed, the results of the information are provided to those who offered the information, to close the loop and show how their input was used. Let's look at these steps in greater detail.

EXHIBIT 7-1
Phase 2: Assessment

△ **Quick-Assessment**
  △ **Self-Assessment**
    △ **Customer Survey**
      △ **Organizational Assessment**
        △ **TQM Planning Inventory**
          △ **Training Feedback**

Quick-Assessment

The Quick-Assessment tool included in Exhibit 7-2 is intended to serve two basic purposes. First, it is used during the first Corporate Council session where the group begins planning the TQM process. Second, it serves as a single tool for the Council to gain valuable insight into the perspectives of company management and workforce.

EXHIBIT 7-2
Example Quick- Assessment

1. What does this company have to do to remain competitive in the future?

2. What do you see as the reason and benefit for TQM?

3. If successful, what would TQM look like in your company? How would you measure it?

4. What are the obstacles to implementing TQM?

5. Who are your customers?

6. How do you determine customer satisfaction?

So how does the Council use the responses in the planning process? Although all six questions are important, I would single out two as being of special interest. The response to question three helps Council members establish their expectations for results and a means for measuring these results. Question four tells you what obstacles, or stumbling blocks, Council members could anticipate in implementing a quality process. This is very important. These issues must be systematically addressed when communicating the purpose, direction, and expectations of senior management in establishing the quality process.

Two points are associated with the tool itself. First, as the name implies it offers a "quick" perspective on the opinions of the individuals being surveyed. Therefore, although it doesn't provide a lot of information to the Council, it serves as a weathervane, allowing them to make basic training decisions in the planning process. Second, it should provide feedback to surveyed individuals as to if, and how, the information was used. As more organizations begin a quality initiative, it is commonplace to blanket the employee in surveys and questionnaires. In essence, employees are surveyed out, so the brevity of this survey brings welcome relief. But the Council must provide feedback to the surveyed individuals, showing that the information was used. This makes the administration of future surveys easier.

Self-Assessment

One tool I like is the Performax Systems International, Inc. Personal Profile System©. It provides a means to better understand our own behavioral patterns and those of other people. It is used most effectively in the early stages of TQM, during team-building exercises. It works extremely well during the first training session for Process Action Teams (PATs).

Behavior patterns include the way we think, feel, and act in our day-to-day environment, and how we respond to new demands and situations. An internationally-recognized expert on the subject of negotiating, Roger Dawson, uses this technique to better understand what turns on and what turns off the person he expects to do business with. Recognizing the four behavior patterns in the Performax System helps both in business endeavors and in making TQM a reality.

We refer to the four basic behavior profiles as D, I, S, and C. Each exhibits certain personality traits that are identifiable to the trained person. By understanding these personalities, you form a more effective TQM team. A high "D" profile person is characterized as a people mover, someone who is impatient. I am a high D. Someone with an "I" personality seeks recognition, is basically disorganized, and resists personal rejection. A person with an "S" personality is a cooperative group worker, possessive, and fearful of risk taking. The "C" personality is creative, fearful of rejection, and resistant to criticism of his/her ideas and work. Because profiles change when people experience stress, they can serve as indicators for times when others feel uncomfortable.

You may be asking yourself, "What does all this have to do with TQM and me?" All teams probably consist of a mix of individuals from each of these four personality types. Your understanding of these different personalities, their strengths and their fears, allows you to form a team more quickly and capitalize on individual strengths. It also moves you toward better process improvement solutions much faster.

My initial focus in TQM has been in the area of technical tools. The first time I used the Performax Personality System was an enlightening experience. I discovered that I possess a strong type-D personality. (Many engineers are D's.) A woman in our group stood up to describe the characteristics typical of D's. She began by saying they were movers and shakers, go-getters, decisive! I felt pretty good about myself. She then continued describing her perception of type-D's. All of a sudden it dawned on me that some of her remarks were not exactly complimentary. In fact, some were downright insulting. The terms "pushy" and "loud" stuck in my mind most. What hurt more was that she was right. Thus the moral of the story: the more you understand yourself and those around you, the better chance you have of getting along with others and working toward a common goal.

Having worked in both private industry and government for a number of years, I have attended more than my share of meetings. When introduced to someone for the first time, something surfaces early in the meeting that tells me whether we will get along famously, or whether something is just not right. TQM training helped me appreciate the personality traits of others. Understanding traits that annoy me enables me to work with people more effectively and ignore personality disconnects that previously hindered our business relationship. It makes good business sense to know about this.

The Personality Profile System by Performax is an excellent tool of TQM. For more information contact:

> Performax Systems International, Inc.
> Attn: Sandra Burk, Sales Administrator
> P.O. Box 59159
> Minneapolis, MN 55459-8247
> (612) 449-2824

Customer Survey

The customer survey provides an important assessment tool. It presents an opportunity to convey your concern for customer satisfaction and your appreciation for their business. How many times have you lost valued customers, only to discover later that some small detail or minor price differences caused them to move to a competitor? The customer survey helps determine exactly what your customer expects from your organiza-tion. Feedback from the customer can take place informally, through conversation, or formally, via surveys or questionnaires. Most often informal feedback is negative. Customers always reserve the right to give you a piece of their mind. People are much more likely to complain when something goes wrong, than to praise you when things go well. But not always.

When Hershey sent Desert Bars to Saudi Arabia, the Army's Chief Food Technologist communicated the troops' enthusiasm back to the corporation. Individuals also responded. One soldier said that after 17 years in the service, the Desert Bar® was the first product he had really enjoyed. A Kansas serviceman wrote to Hershey after reading about the candy in the *Stars and Stripes*. "I have 160 people over here," he explained, "and we haven't gotten our hands on any of these Desert Bars." He even included a picture of himself with his camel out in the middle of nowhere. How could Hershey refuse this request? They sent enough product for his entire battalion.

Exhibit 7-3 provides an example of a formal customer feedback form. My firm used this particular form to administer a customer survey for a professional services firm I'm calling "YOUR" company. While there are many ways to design and administer the survey, I will describe my underlying assumptions, which may be helpful.

First, the form is designed to address some specific areas of interest for the company. Some questions I like to include in any survey form are numbers six through nine. Number ten is a catch-all. Number six asks your client for an overall company rating between one and ten. The response to question seven can be very enlightening, especially for service companies. Whether you receive a very good or not-so-good rating, generally one specific feature of your operation caused the client to give that rating. This information is invaluable.

Question eight asks your client to benchmark your performance with respect to your competitors. Asking this question creates what is called a two-dimensional survey. Not only are you seeking feedback on your individual performance, you are asking how you perform with respect to the competition. This second dimension is very important. I once worked with a company that consistently, over the years, asked their clients how they were performing. And they received very high scores consistently—eights or nines on a scale of one to ten. But when they asked the second dimensional

EXHIBIT 7-3
SAMPLE CUSTOMER SURVEY

1. Describe those attributes you look for in a provider of professional services. _____

   _____

2. What single attribute of a professional services firm conveys their desire to meet your needs? _____

   _____

3. What single factor leads you to believe a professional services firm has begun to take your business for granted? _____

   _____

4. Describe the attributes you find most desirable in a Project Manager you will be coordinating with on a regular basis. _____

   _____

5. Identify any policies of a professional services firm that have historically served as roadblocks to getting the job done. _____

   _____

6. Please provide an overall rating of Y O U R Company performance as a provider of professional services (Please circle one).

   Poor 1   2   3   4   5   6   7   8   9   10   Excellent

7. In one sentence or phrase, please summarize your opinion of Y O U R Company. _____

   _____

8. Please identify the relative performance of Y O U R Company when compared to others offering similar professional services.

   Worse   1   2   3   4   5   6   7   8   9   10   Better

9. Please describe what singular factor caused you give them the above rating. _____

   _____

10. What additional comments or remarks you would like to make that would aid Y O U R Company in better meeting your needs in the future?

    _____

    _____

question, "How are we performing with respect to our competitors?" they discovered important truths. They rated about average—a five on a scale from one to ten. So individually they were top performers, but as a group they were average, not favorable in an industry with only two other competitors in a certain geographic area. The response to question nine allowed them to target certain aspects of their business for improvement. Oftentimes Council members wrestle with the question, "What do we measure in our company to track our performance in the eyes of the customer?" Generally responses to questions seven and nine can shed helpful insight.

Customer feedback can lead to interesting revelations. For instance, sometimes it's not a process that needs to be improved, rather it's the big "C's" *perception* of that process. Sinai Hospital in Detroit encountered such a situation when the responses to a national patient survey showed that their patients believed their bathrooms weren't being cleaned. When the housekeeping staff learned about the survey results, they explained that they generally entered the room quietly and tried to clean the bathroom without disturbing the patients.

Unaware that a staff member was cleaning the bathroom, the patients assumed no one had done the job. So housekeeping tried a new approach. Now they introduce themselves when they enter a room and tell the patient what they will be doing. They also ask whether or not it is a convenient time. The bathrooms are as clean as before, but now the patients rate them as cleaner. This new method has yielded some unexpected benefits, too; comments about the friendliness of the housekeeping staff have increased significantly.

We now have seen examples of both informal and formal customer feedback. So how are they administered? Informal feedback is easy. Either your front-line people solicit this input, or the customer provides it without being asked. Management's challenge is to ensure the information makes it back to the company, so it can be acted upon. While attending the University of New Mexico for my undergraduate degree, a student friend of mine worked for Hewlett-Packard as a sales representative during the summer. He said sales representatives frequently relayed customer suggestions to the company on how to improve the product. Sometimes they were simple suggestions, like moving over a dial on a piece of equipment for easier access. If these suggestions proved out, they would typically surface in the next generation of product.

Administering the formal surveys is a "black art" with lots of suggestions, but few hard-fast, concrete rules. It seems every time I administer a customer survey for a client, something changes. However, my experience shows that surveys should be administered with a personal touch. Mail a copy of the survey to your valued customers, and prompt them in the cover letter by mentioning that someone will call in a week to ten days to get their answers over the phone. This serves many purposes besides adding the personal touch.

First, it allows you to gather feedback that may go beyond the scope of the prepared questions and influence future surveys. Second, we have administered such surveys and have had response rates approaching 100%. This is especially valuable in companies with a small customer base. One client administered his own survey through the mail. But customers did not take time to answer the questions until the quality coordinator personally telephoned and collected their responses. As it turned out, their customers, primarily general contractors, are very busy people who are unaccustomed to such inquiries. So for their second survey, they tried a different approach by offering a $5.00 credit on the next invoice for those completing and returning the survey. This incentive increased their mail-in response from zero to over 65 percent the last time I checked. Quite an improvement!

Second, it is best to have the survey administered by an independent third party. There are two ways to go about doing this. You can hire a consultant, the traditional course of action for many companies. Or you can try an innovative, equally effective approach by contacting a local business school seeking semester projects for hungry students. With so many academic institutions offering TQM and quality-related courses these days, acquiring this talent is a straight-forward process. This works especially well if you have a student on a cooperative education program who can alternate semesters on campus and at your company. There is something disarming about having a young college student call on customers and ask a few pointed questions about the performance of a company. Customers tend to open up.

So how do you decide which customers to survey? I like to send formal surveys to three basic types of customers: (1) existing customers, (2) past customers, and (3) "want-to-be's." Let me explain. In attempting to increase our customer base, it's easy to overlook our "bread and butter," our existing customers. Directing surveys toward them helps reinforce our bond by positively acknowledging them and finding out what they especially like about us. We want to maintain those things we are presently doing right. Surveying past customers helps us understand why we lost their business. Consistent with my earlier remarks about the formal customer survey, the loss of a customer is frequently triggered by one particular thing; sometimes it's something simple. We need to know the reason in order to interrupt the flow of customers to our competitors. The third category, the "want-to-be's" is the most interesting. Much of my own work comes from professional services firms: architectural and engineering services, testing services, government contractors and the like. In response to a depressed economy, my competitors are actively pursuing new customers to help offset revenue losses from existing clients. This is done by approaching business prospects, giving them a customer survey form, and asking them to rate their current provider of goods and services. The response to question nine (Exhibit 7-3) tells you what makes your competitor so special—valuable information indeed. Most of your "want-to-be's" would look forward to providing such feedback, fostering the spirit of healthy competition.

Although you can survey customers anywhere in the TQM improvement process, you should conduct a survey and compile the results before the Corporate Council selects an implementation strategy. At this point, the Council determines the criteria for selecting problems for resolution, and PATs are formed. Customer feedback, a crucial factor, may greatly influence the Council's selection of a strategy. More and more corporate executives have noticed clients demanding higher quality products and services. Once the proper quality is established, then they demand competitive pricing.

Organizational Assessment

Organizational Assessment provides an important mechanism for understanding yourself, your organization, and its members, as a corporate entity. Essentially, it evaluates the current state of an organization, by assessing a multitude of factors, and can lead to positive, action-oriented recommendations for improvement. Factors that contribute to the development of these recommendations include the organization's "vision" of where it wants to be, as well as the customers' expectations. The organizational assessment process can measure and quantify variables, such as an individual's beliefs, that were once considered unmeasurable. Each organization has an individual culture, or climate. Let's look at a couple of examples.

One example we can all relate to is AT&T. In the 1960s and '70s, Bell Laboratories operated from the perspective of a public servant. Yes, they made money, but above all else, they aimed to provide good telephone service to the public. This was really the dominant motivation; the concept of competition never entered into the corporate thinking and planning processes. Then in the early 1980s, several FCC and court decisions began to inject competition into various parts of the business. The biggest blow occurred in 1984, with the divestiture. The introduction of competition changed the corporate culture in a number of ways. For one thing, it resulted in substantial downsizing. Before divestiture, AT&T employed one million people. After divestiture, about 330 thousand AT&T employees remained. Within a few years, the workforce was again reduced to about 250 thousand, and the trend continues.

No longer considered a public servant, AT&T now competes for customers to buy their products and services. As a result, the entire attitude has changed, and a new corporate culture has emerged. Now they must focus on surviving in a competitive marketplace, rather than providing a public service. Naturally, the notion of service remains. (Any corporation that doesn't understand customers and provide some form of public service is likely to fail.) But the type of service has changed radically.

One might think of the parallel between the old-fashioned gas station and the modern version. In the old days, you drove up in your car and rain or shine, an attendant came out and filled your tank, cleaned you windows, and checked your oil. The customer merely gave orders and paid the bill. Now you drive up and do all the work yourself, or pay an extra cost for previously "free" customer service. Some stations even demand payment in advance.

The old-fashioned gas station resembled the old AT&T. Many of the "self-service" elements of the telephone business are no longer the norm, because of price competition. Whether the last vestiges of the old service ethic will vanish or not depends mostly on what people want. But customers will always appreciate good service of some kind, and the business that fails to recognize this will be in immediate jeopardy.

Summit Electric Supply Company devotes the first two days of a person's employment to training about the company culture. New staff members learn the company policies and standards. They also receive an introduction to the corporate culture, as they hear about the company's attitude towards them, and the attitude the company wants to convey to customers. New employees are taught to identify a customer focus with every single job. Everyone—from delivery drivers to counter personnel—contributes to the customers' perception of the company. With an emphasis on serving customers promptly and precisely, Summit expects employees to give 110% at all times. But these high expectations don't deter job applicants; the company receives an average of 200-250 resumes for each person hired.

One assessment tool used throughout the military is the *DoD Quality and Productivity Self-Assessment Guide for Defense Organizations.* Virtually every military department and agency is using it. At latest count, *The Guide* has about 10,000 users worldwide. Of those, 50% are DoD, 30% are domestic agencies, 10% are state and local governments, and 10% are private-sector companies. Many of the private sector companies are defense contractors that cover a full range of Standard Industrial Codes (SIC) which include both service and manufacturing. Even a major cinema is using it.

The *Quality and Productivity Self Assessment Guide* provides an assessment of current practices, procedures and attitudes. Periodic use of *The Guide* gives you an opportunity to assess the effects of any changes as they relate to quality and productivity efforts, stimulates thinking about tools and techniques for quality and productivity enhancement, and helps you discover areas for improvement.

The Guide asks questions about corporate climate, that is, people's perceptions of their organization. These questions address the processes, the organization's policies, procedures and practices; the tools, specific techniques used to promote quality and productivity improvement throughout the organization; and the outcomes, level of mission accomplishment. The status of your organization is confidential, so results and evaluations remain with you and your staff. With this excellent measurement tool you can establish a baseline and measure your progress on an periodic/annual basis. Essentially, you take a snapshot now and try to make it into a motion picture by tracking your progress over time. Although participation should be voluntary, I strongly recommend striving for 100% involvement when administering *The Guide.* If your organization has hundreds or thousands of people, the 100% goal diminishes for practical reasons. There, statistical techniques are used to obtain a significant sampling, yielding a reduced administrative burden with summary results that still have merit.

There are two versions of *The Guide*, one manual and one computerized. In either case, the complete survey takes about thirty to forty minutes to complete. The manual version requires additional time for compilation and calculation of results.

The DoD self-assessment model examines organizational climate and tools for quality improvement, which account for 60% of the variability of the quality outcomes in an organization. A climate for continuous improvement is essential for proceeding into the quality improvement area. If many scores fall below target in the climate, a lot of front-end work must be done before moving into the continuous improvement process. Those results can dramatically influence training budgets for TQM.

Exhibit 7-4 provides a sample output to show how this information is summarized and used in the quality process. This particular climate summary is for federal executive departments and agencies. Baseline data are also available for state and local governments, as well as the private sector. It is important to realize there are no right or wrong scores.

Along the top of the Exhibit we see several columns. Let's look more closely at the Area/Category/Subcategory and Mean columns. The other columns are beyond the scope of this discussion and involve the statistical aspects of the results, *The Guide* provides ample instruction in these areas.

In examining the organizational climate report, consider the Customer Orientation category. This indicates the doubt that people in the organization are "customer" oriented, keeping in mind that this applies to both internal and external customers. Subcategories include Value Systems/Ethics and Communications. The number next to these subcategories appears in the mean column.

The response for Value Systems/Ethics subcategory is 4.26 in the mean column. Considering that guidance and the measurement scale of 1-6, scores less than or equal to 3.5 indicate that conditions typically considered helpful for quality or productivity may be absent in the organization. A mean score of 4.26 is pretty good. Every organization promotes some set of values about people and their work. We're talking about honesty and integrity, the cornerstone of any quality improvement effort. A solid understanding of the strengths of your organization will help you allocate those precious training resources more effectively.

EXHIBIT 7-4
Organizational Climate Report
Consolidated Work Force Scores

Organization: FEDERAL EXECUTIVE DEPARTMENTS & AGENCIES
Work Unit: FEDERAL BASELINE DATA

If any score is lower than or equal to 3.50, it means that some practices typically considered helpful for quality and/or productivity may be absent in your organization. You may want to review the actions/suggestions under the Ideas and Sources option.

Area Category Subcategory	Mean	Standard Deviation	95% Confidence Interval	
Awareness of Strategic Challenge	4.14	0.98	4.04	4.25
Vision for the Future	3.79	0.99	3.69	3.90
Innovation	3.73	1.12	3.61	3.85
Quality Policy/Philosophy	3.74	0.93	3.64	3.84
Value Systems/Ethics	4.26	0.89	4.16	4.36
Strategic Focus	**3.95**	**0.77**	**3.86**	**4.03**
Leader's Involvement	3.90	0.79	3.81	3.98
Leader's Visible Commitment to Goals	4.01	1.05	3.89	4.12
Supervisor's Role in Quality Improvement	4.03	0.89	3.94	4.13
Supervisor's Concern for Improvement	3.63	1.03	3.51	3.74
System/Structure for Quality Improvement	3.65	1.09	3.53	3.77
Leadership and Management	**3.86**	**0.81**	**3.77**	**3.94**
Awareness of Productivity/Quality Issues	3.55	1.09	3.44	3.67
Attitudes/Morale	4.11	1.01	4.01	4.22
Cooperation	3.85	1.03	3.74	3.96
Involvement	4.12	0.97	4.02	4.22
Perceptions of Work Environment	3.94	0.96	3.86	4.04
Social Interactions	4.10	1.25	3.96	4.23
Task Characteristics	3.97	0.99	3.86	4.07
Rewards/Recognition	3.87	1.01	3.76	3.98
Work Force	**3.94**	**0.77**	**3.85**	**4.02**
Customer Orientation	3.70	0.99	3.59	3.81
Customer Orientation	**3.70**	**0.99**	**3.59**	**3.81**
Communications	3.58	1.12	3.46	3.70
Communications	**3.58**	**1.12**	**3.46**	**3.70**
Climate	**3.88**	**0.74**	**3.80**	**3.96**

Number of Questionnaires 336   As of: 04/07/92

Now let's consider the score of 3.58 in the Communications sub-category. This number indicates that organization members may lack the information they need to do their jobs. Although better than the target value of 3.5, it is the lowest scored area. Some actions for improvement may include having representatives hold monthly meetings to exchange information, preparing regular correspondence that disseminates the needed information, and the like.

Understanding an organization's culture, or climate, is an important part of any successful quality process. Organizations overlooking this step in the quality process typically regret it, as they attempt to understand the behavioral changes occurring in the organization as a result of their investment. For more information on the Quality and Productivity Self-Assessment Guide call:

> Government Printing Office
> (202) 783-3238
>
> Ask about stock number 008-000-00619-9.

TQM Planning Inventory

I developed this assessment tool after realizing that the same questions apply to most new clients at the beginning of an assignment. Exhibit 7-5 provides a copy of this form. The left-hand column identifies your current phase in the implementation process along with an itemized inventory list. These inventory items correspond to the steps we take in this book to proceed through the implementation process. For each inventory item, such as Vision Statement, simply "√" the appropriate box to the right—done, in progress, to be done, or not applicable. After completing the inventory, a quick review will shed light on how much you've accomplished thus far, and what still remains to be addressed. Chapter 4 introduced the "Done" and "2-Be-Done" columns in Exhibit 4-3. If you complete this list as part of your first Corporate Council session, you will have essentially completed the TQM Planning Inventory.

Exhibit 7-5

Total Quality Management Planning Inventory (TQMPI)

			Status Items		
Phase / Inventory Item		Done	In Progress	To Be Done	Not Applicable
0.0	**Phase 0: Preparation**				
0.1	**Decision to Consider TQM**	( )	( )	( )	( )
0.2	**Key Executive Training**	( )	( )	( )	( )
0.3	**Assess Need for Consultant**	( )	( )	( )	( )
0.4	**Select Consultant**	( )	( )	( )	( )
0.5	**Strategic Planning**	( )	( )	( )	( )
0.5.1	Vision Statement	( )	( )	( )	( )
0.5.2	Corporate Goals	( )	( )	( )	( )
0.6	**Corporate Quality Policy**	( )	( )	( )	( )
0.7	**Corporate Communication**	( )	( )	( )	( )
0.8	**Decision to Proceed**	( )	( )	( )	( )
1.0	**Phase 1: Planning**				
1.1	**Form Team**	( )	( )	( )	( )
1.2	**Council Training**	( )	( )	( )	( )
1.3	**Identify Expectations for Results**	( )	( )	( )	( )
1.4	**Identify Obstacles**	( )	( )	( )	( )
1.5	**Select TQMCoordinator**	( )	( )	( )	( )
1.6	**Train TQM Coordinator**	( )	( )	( )	( )
1.7	**Strategic Planning (Continued)**	( )	( )	( )	( )
1.7.1	Corporate Objectives	( )	( )	( )	( )
1.7.2	Corporate Tasks	( )	( )	( )	( )
1.7.3	Corporate Performance Measurements	( )	( )	( )	( )
1.8	**Select Approach to Prioritize Processes**	( )	( )	( )	( )
1.9	**Select Processes for Improvement**	( )	( )	( )	( )
1.10	**Bring Support Services on Board**	( )	( )	( )	( )
1.11	**Develop Implementation Schedule**	( )	( )	( )	( )
1.12	**Develop Implementation Budget**	( )	( )	( )	( )
1.13	**Decide to Proceed**	( )	( )	( )	( )

For your FREE, full-sized copy of the TQM Planning Inventory, please call TMC, Inc. at (505) 299-3983.

Exhibit 7-5.

Total Quality Management Planning Inventory (TQMPI) (Cont.)

| Phase / Inventory Item | | Status Items | | | |
		Done	In Progress	To Be Done	Not Applicable
2.0	**Phase 2: Assessment**				
2.1	**Quick-Assessment**	( )	( )	( )	( )
2.2	**Self-Assessment**	( )	( )	( )	( )
2.3	**Customer Survey**	( )	( )	( )	( )
2.4	**Organizational Assessment**	( )	( )	( )	( )
2.5	**TQM Planning Inventory**	( )	( )	( )	( )
2.6	**Training Feedback**	( )	( )	( )	( )
3.0	**Phase 3: Implementation**				
3.1	**Select Support Personnel**	( )	( )	( )	( )
3.2	**Train Support Personnel**	( )	( )	( )	( )
3.3	**Train Management**	( )	( )	( )	( )
3.4	**Train Workforce**	( )	( )	( )	( )
3.5	**Form PATs**	( )	( )	( )	( )
3.6	**PAT Training**	( )	( )	( )	( )
3.7	**Provide Executive Reinforcement**	( )	( )	( )	( )
3.8	**Offer First Success Story**	( )	( )	( )	( )
4.0	**Phase 4: Diversification**				
4.1	**Communication to Suppliers**	( )	( )	( )	( )
4.1.1	Provide Initial Training	( )	( )	( )	( )
4.1.2	Identify Priorities to Select Strategic Suppliers	( )	( )	( )	( )
4.1.3	Modify Competitive Solicitations to Reflect Quality Focus	( )	( )	( )	( )
4.1.4	Certify Suppliers	( )	( )	( )	( )
4.1.5	Begin Supplier Reduction	( )	( )	( )	( )
4.1.6	Provide Ongoing Supplier Support	( )	( )	( )	( )
4.2	**Communication to Subordinate Organizations**	( )	( )	( )	( )
4.2.1	Initial Coordination	( )	( )	( )	( )
4.2.2	Initial Training	( )	( )	( )	( )
4.2.3	Ongoing Subordinate Organization Support	( )	( )	( )	( )
4.3	**Networking**	( )	( )	( )	( )

So how are these results used? The "Done" list acknowledges your current accomplishments. The other checked items will either become implementation schedule line items, or they are not applicable to your organization. Both results bear special meaning, if customers or clients are already asking for information about your quality process. This simple form saves everyone several hours in developing a better understanding of an organization's status in the quality process. I believe you will find it a useful tool, regardless of where you are in your TQM initiative.

Training Feedback

Training feedback comprises the sixth and final step of the Assessment phase. By the time you receive your first training survey, the organization's training department will have invested a lot of time in selecting and scheduling training. This is your first opportunity to view the perceptions of the training attendees and to evaluate the impact your investment has had on the bottom line.

Exhibit 7-6 shows a sample training survey. Although it is only an example, like the customer survey, it should address two basic questions: "How did we do?" and "How can we improve?" If initial training for managers or the workforce has been ineffective, you'll need time to make the necessary course adjustments using these survey results. I have seen training critiques several pages long, and some that encompass less than a page. I prefer a shorter format, because it can be completed in less than a minute, as someone runs out the door. People with more specific concerns generally take the opportunity to elaborate in the margins and spaces provided.

Obtaining surveys following each training session should be routine, with the results being compiled and summarized by the training department representative and the TQM Coordinator. The Council also needs to know the results of these surveys, since training represents one of the largest financial commitments of the decision to proceed into Phase 3, Implementation.

EXHIBIT 7-6
Example Training Feedback

1. Overall reaction to coverage of subject material:
   Please circle one   (Poor) 1   2   3   4   5   (Best)

2. Overall reaction to applicability of material covered to your company:
   Please circle one   (Poor) 1   2   3   4   5   (Best)

3. Overall reaction to instructor's delivery of topic material:
   Please circle one   (Poor) 1   2   3   4   5   (Best)

4. What material covered today proved most useful for you?

   _____

   _____

5. What material presented today was of little value to you?

   _____

   _____

6. General Comments:

   _____

   _____

Other Assessments

The list of potential tools an organization might use to establish channels of communication is endless. But one commonly used approach in America that deserves special attention is the Malcolm Baldrige National Quality Award criteria. In Chapter 3, I explained that while the number of applicants for the prize has not changed dramatically since its inception in 1988, the number of Criteria Booklets being mailed has increased twenty times. So the Malcolm Baldrige criteria can serve as an organization-wide assessment of where you are in the quality process. Like the organizational assessment described above, there are no right or wrong answers. But knowing your strengths and deficiencies helps you better allocate precious resources to the improvement process more effectively.

> *"We have adopted the Baldrige criteria as our road map.*
> *The benefit is getting and keeping customers better than*
> *our competitors."*

> Robert Shafto
> CEO
> The New England

Chapter 8. Phase 3: Implementation

Overview

We have finally arrived! After Preparation, Planning and Assessment, we reach that point where we will see a return on our investment of time and money. This is Phase 3, Implementation. Here the organization's support personnel are selected and trained; managers and workforce personnel are trained; PATs are put in place and if all goes well, you begin to see results. Exhibit 8-1 summarizes the steps necessary to accomplish implementation. Each step is described later in detail.

EXHIBIT 8-1
Phase 3: Implementation

△ Select Support Personnel
  △ Train Support Personnel
    △ Management Training
      △ Workforce Training
        △ Form PATs
          △ PAT Training
            △ Executive Reinforcement
              △ First Success Story

Select and Train Support Personnel

Step 1 involves the selection of the organization's support personnel, which include facilitators, trainers and internal consultants. These important people will maintain high-visibility positions within the organization, as an extension of the TQM Coordinator and an integral part of Support Services.

Facilitators and trainers will undergo training similar to that of the Coordinator. This includes problem-solving skills, meeting conduct skills, and a mixture of both technical and non-technical tools as described in Exhibit 6-6 in Chapter 6. Internal consultants, and sometimes trainers, may receive facilitator training, but not always. Typically, these people bring a specialized skill to the TQM process.

For example, I conducted training for an office of the U.S. Geological Survey. As we progressed through introductory training (Awareness Training) and elaborated on the skills we would need to move forward, the topic of statistics came up. We soon discovered that someone in the audience had completed several undergraduate and graduate courses on the subject, and regularly applied the concepts at work. There was our statistics trainer! This person, though not seeking to facilitate meetings or manage conflict, has valuable expertise to share as a trainer.

Internal consultants are mentors within the organization who consult on a one-on-one basis or in small groups. An internal consultant could be the statistical specialist I just described. Most likely, these will include individuals who have just completed a PAT, and by applying such skills as flow charting, measurement, and design of data sheets, have become the resident experts in these areas. As PAT training proceeds, "specialists" emerge. Each person begins to identify with those topics he or she feels most comfortable with. Some will gravitate toward the more technical tools, such as control charts. Others may focus on presentation skills or conducting personality profile exercises. No matter. The TQM Coordinator will schedule these personnel, using the strengths and specialized skills of each. Everyone can contribute.

So as you can see, some of these positions, such as facilitators, require new training. People learn a great deal as they proceed through PAT training and practice these skills. In other instances, as in the case of the statistician, people who have already acquired specialized skills from any number of sources can share this expertise with their co-workers. TQM provides the vehicle for bringing this talent to the front of the room.

Management and Workforce Training

Steps 3 and 4 involve training management and workforce personnel. This area presents problems for many companies. Group or large-scale training should begin only after completing the necessary planning, selecting the terminology you will use, and propagating executive momentum throughout the organization. If you follow this approach, you can proceed on solid footing.

Large companies, with hundreds of thousands of employees, face the dilemma of where to begin quality training. Wal-Mart started its formal quality training program right in the home office, with the 4,000 associates in Bentonville, Arkansas. Top management realized that the problems they faced were opportunities for improvement, so they started by orienting the home office associates to quality issues, with particular emphasis on developing sensitivity to the little "c"—the internal customer. With that process in place, they began working with the stores and distribution centers, weaving in the concepts of quality and introducing teams.

Exhibit 8-2 outlines a road map for the kinds of training each employee will receive. I divide training into three basic categories: (1) Awareness Training, (2) Orientation Training, and (3) Skills Training. Like the pieces of a puzzle, each plays a specific role, critical to transitioning all employees toward Total Quality. The most valuable aspect of my training approach is timing. Each session provides employees with enough information so they can digest it, discover which facets of TQM they agree with, and identify those parts of TQM they simply do not believe. That's fine. A later training session will address these concerns. All issues are real, and they are dealt with directly in open forums.

EXHIBIT 8-2
Corporate-Wide Training to Support TQM Implementation

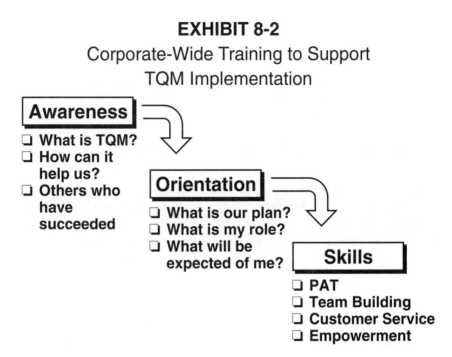

Awareness training is the first exposure your people will have to TQM. This pivotal introduction plants the seed that TQM has helped other companies and can successfully be applied here. Most important, it should be brief—fifty minutes maximum. This presentation should be polished, well-organized, and prepared to address basic concepts: (1) What is Total Quality Management? (2) Who has benefited? and (3) How can it help you? If the necessity of TQM is not yet apparent, explain that quality is a survival mechanism for the company (and the country) in order to compete and prosper in the existing and developing world economy. The need for this additional explanation may become evident after compiling results from the self-evaluation in Phase 2. Everyone must believe that a need to improve the way we do business exists, and that TQM is a proven vehicle for accomplishing that goal.

I recently presented a series of Awareness Training sessions to one organization. Managers were anxious to implement TQM, streamline processes, and change the world. Although they focused upon using rather sophisticated technical tools of TQM, it was evident that they could achieve great returns in the short-term by applying simpler techniques. For example, I realized (as did probably everyone who tried to call them) that their telephone skills were abysmal. It was commonplace for the telephone to ring five, and sometimes ten times before someone would answer it. I mention this because all too often, executives and managers pursue complex solutions to commonplace problems and in doing so, overlook the basics. Yes, much of the training your people obtain through TQM reemphasizes the basics: team building, group dynamics, and of course, let's not overlook telephone techniques.

Orientation Training will be longer—about three to four hours. Here, each employee learns of the company's strategic plan to make Total Quality a way of life. All of the planning that has been invested thus far is unveiled for all to see. To a corporate executive, this represents reward time. As such, a senior person within the company should play a key role in the presentation. Beyond discovering the magnitude of the changes taking place, each employee should understand a handful of key points. (1) There is top-level commitment. They know that because you are present, in the flesh, telling them. (2) Everyone in the organization will be affected in a positive fashion. If something about your job causes you dissatisfaction, now is the time to improve it. (3) Everyone contributes in this process. Employees who have not already volunteered to become a facilitator or trainer should know they will have many other opportunities to participate. (4) Finally, they receive a schedule of what can be expected and when. There will be no surprises, and everyone will know what is happening. They will be kept abreast of chartered PATs and recognized for their progress and contributions toward making TQM a reality.

Specific skills training comprises the third element in the training process. We've already discussed the generic training presented to everyone in the company. Here, I will describe specific training. This can include leadership training, presentation skills training, telephone answering skills, etc. Sound familiar? That's right, much of the skills training represents a continuation of the already planned and budgeted training initiatives. The difference is that TQM will relate it to the organization's corporate strategic plan, based on a determination of needs. These needs become apparent as opportunities for improvement surface during the Assessment Phase. Remember, the goal of all this training is to have your people practice these skills as continuous process improvement becomes a routine course of doing business. It should integrate into the corporate culture as employees buy-into the TQM process.

Process Action Team Training

Probably the most obvious, focused, TQM training for a company is Process Action Team (PAT) training. This training serves as the "meat and potatoes" component of your entire TQM effort. It yields the results—the success stories—you have been looking for. PAT training consists of the five basic parts described in Exhibit 8-3: (1) Introduction and Overview, (2) Information Gathering, (3) Analysis and Interpretation, (4) Packaging and Presentation, and (5) Follow-up. The sequencing and timing of these training events are crucial.

EXHIBIT 8-3
Skills Training to Support TQM Implementation

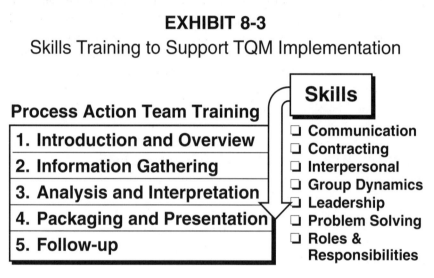

Just as timing is vital in presenting Awareness and Orientation Training to all employees, the timing of each component of PAT training is also important. Each component should give trainees just enough information to do something. That means, provide people enough skills training so they can go forth and practice these skills with some mechanism in place for addressing questions and refining concepts as they proceed. Each PAT and PAT member should have access to a specialist who addresses specific problems as they arise. The TQM Coordinator will make this support available; it consists of a mix of in-house and hired talent. In the course of training, PAT members learn both technical and non-technical tools, which they will apply through a structured problem-solving approach.

Shewhart Cycle

There are many models for continuous process improvement. AT&T uses
Process Quality Management & Improvement (PQMI). Another organization uses the eight-step problem-solving model. A main post office I toured
recently displayed a huge circle on the wall of the training room entitled "12-
Step Problem-Solving Method." One model I use for problem solving, or
continuous improvement, is the Shewhart Cycle shown in Exhibit 8-4. It
includes four quadrants—four parts to improve processes: Plan (P), Do (D),
Check (C), and Act (A).

EXHIBIT 8-4
Shewhart Cycle

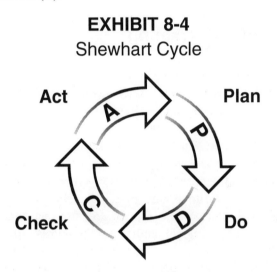

P represents the beginning, early planning. Using the tools of TQM to
identify an opportunity for process improvement, we define the problem,
identify the customers, and understand what quality characteristic is important for the process under study. Then we develop solutions to improve the
process. When one solution is approved, we prepare a schedule and resource
estimates for implementing the quality process. Employees are trained to
smooth the transition to the new, improved process. In D, or Do, we implement
the process improvement with the support of the Corporate Council.

Next is Check, or C. After implementing the new process, we must identify what actually happened. During P, we developed expectations as to how the process would perform after changes were implemented. Now we measure the same things and compare them against the original, or benchmarked, values.

Last is Act, or A. Here, we incorporate successful process improvements as a work standard. This success is applied to other similar processes, and we address the question, "What should we do next?" This presents the first opportunity to communicate success to our people, subordinate organizations and suppliers.

Five Parts of PAT Training

During the first part of PAT training, Introduction and Overview, employees receive training in small groups. Each team consists of four to eight individuals who will be trained to address a specific process identified for improvement by the Corporate Council. These processes may have been selected in several ways. They may have resulted from a brainstorming session with corporate executives, a problem that surfaced during the Organizational Assessment, an employee survey, or customer complaint. I cannot overemphasize the importance of training each group as a team. PAT training provides the initial occasion for creating that bond which will develop among cross-functional entities within your company. Forming this team allows everyone to get special treatment and play a key role in making something positive happen. Teamwork allows team members to fulfill their potential.

Early in the first training session the team will select a recorder, a minute taker, and team leader. The recorder assists the facilitator by summarizing the group's ideas on a flip-chart or wall board. Although this function can be handled by the facilitator, having the assistance of a recorder does speed things up. The minute taker documents the progress of team meetings and training sessions and issues meeting minute notes to team members and the TQM Coordinator. Sometimes the recorder and minute taker are the same person. The team leader schedules and conducts team meetings, schedules training sessions, and represents the PAT before the Corporate Council. The team leader doesn't necessarily represent the highest-ranking individual on the PAT.

The skills taught during Introduction & Overview include team building, brainstorming, and understanding processes. Participants learn basic skills that allow them to work together more effectively. The Performax Personality System provides a tool for assessing personality strengths and weaknesses. Flow charting serves as the most fundamental means for teaching participants how to understand processes. This powerful tool graphically depicts all of the steps, activities, or operations necessary to accomplish the process. It is a simple technique, easily understood by people with very diverse experience and educational backgrounds. As a result of my training, one person, whom I will call Paul, used flowcharts to communicate to a prospective client how the pieces of a software project could be assembled over time to yield a tremendous capability in the long-term, while offering the customer small, incremental improvements in capability in the short-term. He got the job! After completing Part One of PAT training, participants will be armed to work toward process improvement as a team, flow charting their process.

After completing their flow charts, the PATs return to the classroom for the second part of their training—Information Gathering. Here, they use the flow chart to brainstorm opportunities for information that would allow them to quantify the performance of the existing process. In sessions like this, specialized areas of expertise come to light. Clearly, some individuals will shine, having the groups arrive at a list of priorities—brainstormed alternatives. Others will feel more comfortable describing data availability, explaining how that information can most easily be obtained, and identifying ways to compile the information for later use. Everyone can play this role. Upon completing Part 2 of PAT training, each team will be able to gather and summarize the researched information in preparation for the next training session.

The measurement part of the team effort cannot be overemphasized. This frequently determines whether teams will move to a solution very quickly, or stretch out over time. I once trained and facilitated two teams for the Navajo tribe in New Mexico. One team focused on the Payroll Process, which conveniently offered a continuous stream of new information every payroll period, every two weeks. The other team, a Survey PAT, studied ways to improve the surveying process which supported new road construction. The process itself, including the draft, review, and approval cycles, spanned six months or more—far less convenient than that of the Payroll PAT. So information and the availability of this information are very important to the TQM process. They also support a basic principle of TQM, fact-based decision making.

Sometimes we have to abandon the traditional approaches to improve our methods of doing business. For example, the Environmental Protection Agency (EPA), whose business it is to make decisions, used to rely on "best engineering" or "best technical" judgement to plan data collection. But because this method failed to consider what decision the data would support, or the intended use of the data, it had several inherent pitfalls. For instance, you might be measuring the wrong thing; and even if you measure the right thing, you may spend more money than necessary, because you don't know what the data will be used for.

To remedy this problem, the EPA developed a quality assurance program, a "data quality objectives process," to provide performance measures for data collection in the planning stage of new projects. These performance measures determine the amount and type of data needed in advance. They also incorporate a built-in stopping rule, to avoid collecting superfluous data and focus the effort clearly on the problem at hand. Superfund, the EPA's program for the clean up of abandoned waste sites, has applied this methodology at a number of sites around the country and has met with amazing results. For instance, at a Missouri farm contaminated by dioxin, the data quality objectives process led to a more effective, focused remedy, for $6 million less than the projected amount for the traditional method.

Part 3 of PAT training is Analysis and Interpretation. Here, we review the information gathered since the last training session. Participants learn skills that allow them to extract usable information from their data, while applying some basic tools of TQM. These might include a simple tubular compilation of the data, a Pareto Diagram, a control chart, or any number of tools made available to the new problem-solving professionals. These basic tools will be used in preparation for Part 4 of PAT training. Oftentimes the information is presented several different ways for Part 4 training, to develop the best, most concise method for presentation to the Corporate Council.

Part 4, Packaging and Presentation, is where the labors of PAT members come to fruition. Here, the results of analysis and interpretation are reviewed, the information summarizing the best efforts documented for review by the TQM Coordinator, and a brief summary of recommendations prepared for presentation during the next Corporate Council meeting. Remember, this presentation is a sales pitch; this section of PAT training prepares participants to deliver it. Hence, the training includes practicing the presentation with hand-drawn overhead transparencies or a flip chart. When PATs leave this forum, they are ready to "sell" their ideas. Aside from any visual or graphic support, all is done. They are ready. Exhibit 8-5 includes a sample PAT report outline. I like to keep its length at ten pages or less, plus data and analysis charts. When the PAT disbands, the TQM Coordinator keeps this report so others with similar or related processes can benefit from it in the future.

Part 5 of PAT training is Follow-Up. In one instance, a team of six members proceeded to implement the approved recommendations of the Corporate Council. After implementing the recommendations, the team dropped all but two members to monitor the performance of the process improvement one week per month for the next few months. PAT members should realize that their work is not done once the Council has bought-off on their recommendation. Most often they will also implement and monitor the improvement. This feedback is very important to them individually. Instilling self-confidence in their use of these skills helps surface in-house consultants, trainers, or facilitators.

Executive Reinforcement at the Right Time

OK, you have a PAT understanding a process, analyzing data—everything seems to be going well and then it strikes—Failure! What happened? What escaped you? Here we observe a common phenomenon. I call it the attitude cycle, shown in Exhibit 8-6, and it plays a significant role in management's ability to maintain momentum in the TQM initiative. As time goes by, PATs experience certain things in moving from the left of the attitude cycle to the right. How you, as an executive, respond to certain indicators midway through this cycle directly influences whether a particular PAT succeeds or fails. Let's look at an example.

It's the first day of PAT training. A number of your people are in a room, eagerly awaiting this introductory session. As the first hour leads to the wrap-up, everyone is enthusiastic, ready to do great things. They are pumped up. I call it "Uninformed Optimism." Yes, the training adequately prepares them for the tasks at hand, but other forces are at work—forces that will determine the ultimate success or failure of their efforts.

EXHIBIT 8-5
Sample Process Action Team
Report Outline Cover

I. OVERVIEW

    A. Executive Statement

    B. Team Purpose

        1. To make recommendations based on data collected and analyzed

        2. To ask for concurrence from Corporate Council

        3. To continue to review and improve

II. INTRODUCTION (Background)

    A. Brief History

    B. Process Action Team Members

    C. PAT Objectives

III. PROCESS SELECTION

    A. Selection Process

        1. Brainstorming

        2. Flow Chart

        3. Cause & Effect Diagrams

    B. Project Description

IV. PROJECT IMPLEMENTATION

    A. What Data Collected?

    B. Where Data Collected?

    C. When Data Collected?

    D. How Data Collected?

    E. Who Collected Data?

V. ANALYSIS AND RECOMMENDATIONS

    A. Process Changes

    B. Cost Savings

VI. CONTINUING IMPROVEMENTS

    A. PAT Schedule

    B. PAT Recommendations

    C. PAT Follow-up

EXHIBIT 8-6
Maintaining Momentum

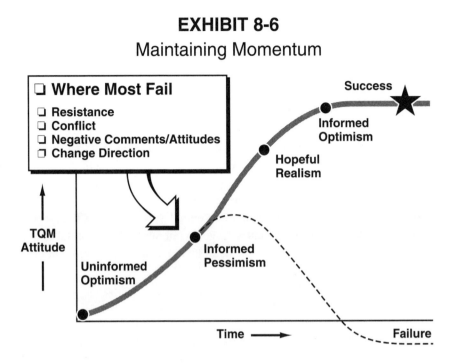

© ODR, Inc., Atlanta, Georgia

When people complete their first training session, they will begin to understand their process, usually through flow charting. They will be the first to gain this insight. And because they are the first, their challenge exceeds that of future PATs. When they solicit support and show enthusiasm for the process, they will probably encounter many disbelievers. At that stage, the PATs reach a mode I call "Informed Pessimism." Others have taken the wind out of their sails; they begin to believe that corporate change is too difficult, maybe even impossible. They require reinforcement, and that is where you come in. Your visible support, your presence in PAT coordination meetings, and your verbal reinforcement when greeting these special people in the halls, help them overcome the slump and press on to success.

If you feel you are too busy, or the task too basic for someone of your stature, the PAT will undoubtedly fail. As Exhibit 8-6 shows, failure takes you below where you had been before as a company in your "TQM Attitude." Can this really be true? After investing your time, energy and money in the process, can you really be worse off than if you had done nothing? The answer is yes. And chances are, if some people offer significant resistance to the quality process, they are probably a remnant of a previously failed management initiative.

In Chapter 4, I describe management commitment. The most valuable commodity you have to offer your PAT members is time. They want to know who is driving the boat, and they want visible evidence of that support. Applying your precious time to these critical instances is essential and will propel your people through "Hopeful Realism," "Informed Optimism," and eventually lead to success. Everyone on the PAT needs your support at key points in the process of improvement. Eventually, previous PAT members will supply this aid, but in the early stages, your support is invaluable and your rewards immeasurable. People at all levels in an organization quickly recognize this type of support.

Have you ever overheard employees talking about their boss? Lots of grumbling goes on, right? "He has no idea how hard we work," or "She couldn't care less about us." Though this scenario can be true, I once overheard an exceptionally moving conversation between two Wal-Mart associates several weeks after the death of the company president.

Standing in front of the greeting cards, I heard two associates talking as they stocked shelves on the next isle. An older woman, helping a new associate, spoke about the company—providing an informal orientation into the corporate culture. As she talked about the passing of the company's founder, her voice quivered. "We had a special day honoring him," she said, "but we didn't close the store. We knew how Mr. Sam would have wanted it—the customer always comes first."

"He was a great man," she continued. "I always looked forward to his visits to Albuquerque. I even have an autographed picture of him," she added with noticeable pride. This woman—one of 380,000 WalMart associates— spoke of Sam Walton with fondness and affection, as though he had been a close personal friend. Highly visible in all his stores, Mr. Sam fostered a spirit of cooperation among the associates. No matter how large an organization, there's no substitute for face-to-face contact. Communication—talking, listening and taking action—makes all the difference in associates' perception of top management.

First Success Story

Part 5 of PAT training, Follow-up, is reward time, as experienced PAT members brief new PAT members during the early stages of their training. In this rewarding experience, newcomers to TQM receive real-world feedback from their peers on the challenges and accomplishments encountered only months earlier. Even not-so-pleasant experiences are valuable, as everyone in the room learns how to overcome an adverse situation that may arise again. Using good project management practices, the PAT anticipates results after a certain period of time. We base the measure of success upon how close the PATs come to meeting the expectations they, themselves, had developed in the P part of the Shewhart Cycle. Another measure, probably more important, is the learning experience taking place. Although we want success stories early on, we also need an education and an understanding of the pitfalls encountered and how to overcome such adversity. Yes, the excellent companies celebrate failure almost as much as they celebrate success. In doing so, they remove employees' hesitation about venturing into the unknown. Whether successful or not, PAT members should know they have the full support of the Corporate Council and the encouragement to participate in the future, regardless of the past. We all have to learn.

How Much Training Is Required?

At this point, you might be thinking, "Gee, this seems like a lot of training, what's all this going to cost?" Chapter 11 describes how to address this point. For now, it is important to review the magnitude of training realized by each level within the organization. You'll find these results summarized in Exhibit 8-7. While the specifics differ for each company, I believe the allocation of training to be widely applicable. As you can see, the training process involves everyone.

Awareness and Orientation training represents only a small fraction of the training each company employee will accomplish. Note that the majority of the time, hence the majority of training resources, is allocated to specific skills training. Again, this emphasizes the need for analyzing and interpreting the results from the Assessment Phase to spend dollars most effectively.

EXHIBIT 8-7

Estimated Initial Training Requirements Necessary to Implement TQM

Layer within Organization	Principles & Concepts	Management Overview	Technical Overview	Specific Skills
Executive	2	2	.5	Days – Weeks
Management	1.5	1.5	.5	Days – Weeks
Workforce	1	.5	.5	Days – Weeks

* All Estimates Are Measured in Days of Training

Training is a key element in making TQM work. Everyone in the company must realize that their turn will come in the training process, and that they will be expected to contribute.

For example, at Summit Electric Supply Company, every employee receives training. Summit devotes between 5% to 7% of an employee's time to training, and some people receive considerably more. Through a Total Quality Process (TQP) system, Summit trains employees in using the basic tools of process improvement, identifying ever-changing customer requirements, and obtaining customer feedback.

Additionally, the company teaches its staff about the products through the use of hard and soft tools. A hard tool, for example would be a measurement, such as having the counter people check the computer printout regularly to see the time that elapses between placing the order and having it ready to pick up. The soft tool involves teaching everyone in the system about Summit products and services. At the counter, for instance, an employee should be able to look at an order, determine what additional supplies might be required, and ask the customer if he needs them. Beyond boosting sales, this extra reminder can save the customer time and frustration—especially if the job site is 40 miles away.

In contrast to many of its competitors, Summit makes a large investment in recruiting new employees, in an effort to hire career-oriented people who will contribute their intelligence and creativity. The company continues to invest in its employees by providing training in areas ranging from product knowledge and technical expertise to interpersonal communication. All employees receive basic TQP training, and some go on to attend quality seminars and specific job-related courses. The payback for this extensive training comes in increased productivity, high morale, and low employee turnover. Summit personnel take pride in working for this successful company.

U.S. companies invest an average of 1.4% of payroll dollars in training that typically reaches only 10% of the workforce. Japanese and European-owned companies based in the U.S. spend 3-5 times and more on employee training than American companies do. Cutting training expenditures today widens the gap with our competitors.

Tools to Aid in Process Improvement

There are many tools one might use to aid in continuous process improvement. One very basic tool I see almost all PATs use is flow charting. Exhibit 8-8 provides a sample flow chart. The process under study is printing a book. Although a very simple example, it communicates a few basic points. For one thing we "see" the basic flow of work; in this case it is paper. The process begins with the customer submitting the work to the printer and ends when the completed book is delivered to the customer. Even in this single process, a lot of things occur. As in the case with manufacturing a product, every time you pass hardware, paper, or information from one step to another, there is an opportunity for a disconnect, an error. "Seeing" the process on paper makes it much easier for the team to understand the process and identify where measurements could be made.

To date, most software packages that aid in process improvement have been written for the technocrat. Difficult to use and unforgiving for the user, they require an extensive background in statistics. This need not be the case.

EXHIBIT 8-8
Example Flow Chart-Printing a Book

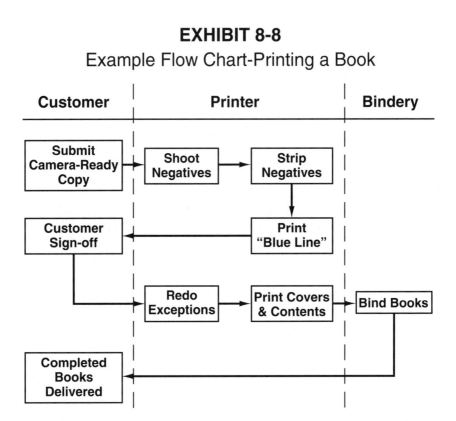

Recent developments by MORE, Inc., a software firm in Albuquerque, New Mexico, have resulted in an easy-to-use, user-friendly, software program to aid PAT participants, called "The Tools of Total Quality Management." Some examples of its capabilities are described below.

Exhibit 8-9 depicts a simple Cause and Effect (C&E) diagram using an administrative example. It allows the PAT, through brainstorming, to identify the events or causes that result in an undesirable outcome. In this example the effect, to the right of the diagram, is "meetings take too long." Typically we focus our attention on this outcome and pay little attention to its cause. Hence, the need for the structured approach to problem solving we discussed earlier. TQM teaches us to identify the cause of this undesirable outcome so we can resolve it.

The administrative example described in Exhibit 8-9 was created by a recorder on a PAT. Basic information, such as title and effect, is completed for the C&E diagram. The diagram summarizes main-cause categories,

EXHIBIT 8-9
Application of Cause & Effect Diagram

Meetings Take too Long – C&E Diagram

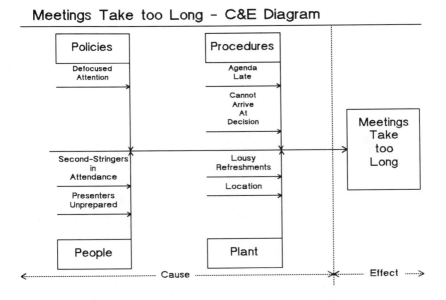

© MORE, Inc., 1992

such as policies, procedures and brainstormed causes for meetings taking too long; an additional column in the software documents comments. These comments provide supplemental information for the PAT member presenting a status report to the Corporate Council. Information is easy to enter with user-friendly, "pop-up" screens that aid in construction of both the input table and subsequent C&E diagrams. In addition, after being transferred to Pareto Chart format, this table becomes a simple check sheet to aid in gathering data.

Exhibit 8-10 shows an example of a Pareto Chart. It provides a simple means to portray data graphically and assist PAT members in prioritizing alternatives. In this case, a show of hands provided a quantified measure for all the possible causes for the meeting taking too long. The data, or show of hands, are logged onto the check sheet, input into the computer, and graphed to produce the results you see in this Exhibit. The tallest column, to the left of the graph, shows how time might be spent overcoming the predominant cause brainstormed during a C&E diagramming session. The results are graphic, easy to understand, and formatted suitably for presentation in open forum, or as documentation of a data analysis function in the PAT report. Utilitarian in nature, the Pareto Chart is applied in most all PATs.

EXHIBIT 8-10
Application of Pareto Chart

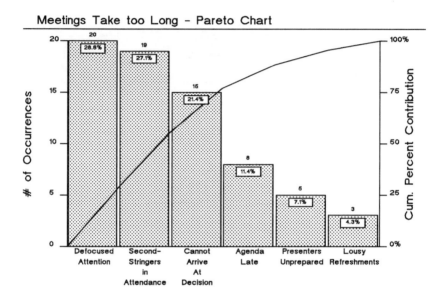

Beyond the simple C&E diagram and Pareto Chart described above, the MORE package offers many other capabilities that ease administrative and presentation burdens of PAT members. These include histograms, run charts, control charts, and others. MORE has an excellent reputation for producing reliable, usable products. For information on "The Tools of Total Quality Management," contact:

MORE, Inc.
7208 Jefferson NE
Suite A
Albuquerque, NM 87109
(505) 344-1233
FAX (505) 344-7079

Professional Affiliations for Assistance

The question often arises, "Where do I go for assistance on Total Quality Management?" At several points throughout this book, I have discussed the use of consultants and suggested several sources for training and consulting support. But what information outlets exist for the TQM Coordinator, the in-house consultant, or the company facilitator? I recommend three basic sources of information and will share two examples of emerging community support activities. Three "must buy" sources for the aspiring TQM enthusiast are from: The American Society for Quality Control (ASQC), The Association for Quality and Participation (AQP) and the Institute for Industrial Engineers (IIE).

The ASQC offers a monthly magazine, *Quality Progress*. Technical libraries usually have *Quality* on their shelves. If you thumb through several issues, you'll find an abundance of relevant information for the quality professional on topics ranging from corporate strategy for improving quality, to the specific use of tools for measuring and improving processes. When first introduced to *Quality Progress*, I copied articles from the library edition so I could read them at my leisure. I realized that I was copying so much information that I joined the ASQC—just to receive the magazine. *Quality Progress* is a must for every quality professional. For more information about the ASQC, contact:

American Society for Quality Control
611 E. Wisconsin Ave.
Milwaukee, WI 53201
(800) 248-1946

And be sure to request a copy of their most recent book catalog. They undoubtedly will have one or two available for your specific circumstance, whether in finance, health care, or heavy industrial manufacturing.

The Association for Quality and Participation (AQP), a 7,500-member non-profit professional association, is an excellent resource for information about quality and participative management. AQP publishes a bi-monthly newsletter and a magazine, *The Journal for Quality and Participation*. Contributors to *The Journal* have included Joseph Juran, Philip Crosby, Armand Feigenbaum and Tom Peters. *The Journal* has also featured special issues for aerospace, health care, communications, government and labor.

AQP sponsors three annual conferences. A typical conference session might showcase NASA's benchmarking techniques, or detail how to implement high-performance compensation systems. AQP also carries over 150 titles of books, audio, software packages and video programs. AQP members have access to a research center with a lending library, and an 80-chapter and regional network spanning the U.S. and Canada. For more information about the AQP, contact:

> Association for Quality and Participation
> 801-B W. 8th Street, Suite 501
> Cincinnati, OH 45203
> (513) 381-1959

I also like the *IIE Monthly Magazine*, an invaluable source for the quality professional. Don't let the title mislead you—it is not just for engineers. I once found an excellent article on how to quantify costs and benefits associated with hospital out-patient care, which I use as an example in workshops on quality in service organizations. This is not the type of material you would generally expect to see in a professional engineering magazine. Their editing is good, the articles brief and to the point, and most important, they have plenty of visuals for describing key concepts.

Another excellent article I read in *IIE Monthly Magazine* related to the use of an electronics spreadsheet as an aid in planning an office reorganization. It explained who should be located where, and how support equipment should be placed for effective utilization. I like this example because everyone goes through this sort of experience sooner or later. For more information about the Institute of Industrial Engineers, contact:

> Institute of Industrial Engineers
> 25 Technology Park/Atlanta
> Norcross, GA 30092
> (404) 449-0460

Now, as promised, I'll provide two examples of TQM community support groups, which are becoming more popular: The Delaware Valley Industrial Resource Center (DVIRC) in Philadelphia, Pennsylvania, and The Sloan School of Management at the Massachusetts Institute of Technology (MIT).

Delaware Valley Industrial Resource Center

According to the *Business Week* article, "You've Got a Friend in PA," Delaware Valley Industrial Resource Center (DVIRC) is one of the leading economic development groups in the country. In its fourth year of operation, DVIRC provides economically feasible approaches for small to mid-size manufacturers entering the world-class arena through the use of TQM.

When considering TQM implementation, small manufacturing companies received proposals from consultants that far exceed their economic range. So DVIRC used the approach described in this book to design a system for smaller manufacturers, for about $32,000. This product walks the clients through from Phase 0, establishing key benchmarks, to Phase 5, providing continuity and maintaining the TQM process. It is modeled after the Five-Phase Approach™ described here, adding a fifth phase to maintain the process.

The company chooses the benchmarks, the things management wants to focus on for improvement, then measures the factors selected in Phase 0 at the onset, after six months, and again after one year. Sometimes manufacturers recognize weaknesses in their own operations and seek to improve their processes voluntarily. But according to Barry Miller, Director of Manufacturing Services of DVIRC, 95 percent of the people who come to the agency regarding TQM are being driven by external forces—whether to meet the expectations of their suppliers or to keep up with the competition.

And the demand for this type of support is increasing. Three years ago DVIRC received about five requests for TQM; 20-25 manufacturers requested it the second year; 38-40 the third; and presently around 60 manufacturers have requested TQM training. This enthusiastic response has convinced DVIRC of the need to provide such services for all manufacturers and to reduce the barriers for them to implement TQM in their organization. I believe they serve as an example of how other local community groups will form to assist small companies in their pursuit of TQM.

Massachusetts Institute of Technology

Academia has joined in industry's movement to TQM by offering courses and programs on this subject. In a recent conversation with Dr. Stephen Graves, a professor and Deputy Dean at the Sloan School of Management, I felt encouraged to hear all the ways MIT is supporting the American quality movement. On the subtlest level, you'll find TQM concepts infused into ongoing courses, such as Statistical Process Control (SPC).

For more comprehensive exposure, MIT recently offered a symposium for companies to get together and share experiences about TQM. The program included presentations from several 1991 Quality Award winners and workshops covering topics such as mobilization, defining customer requirements, Taguchi Methods, and benchmarking.

MIT also offers a graduate-level course on TQM. A visiting professor from Japan who was hired to design and develop this program teaches students about TQM principles, skills and tools. As added reinforcement, the management school, itself, practices TQM, illustrating the concepts in the way it does business.

Students can also earn credit for participating in a workshop, where students, staff, and faculty learn problem-solving and continuous-improvement skills together. Then they form teams and apply the tools to a particular problem within the Sloan School—such as how to enhance the classroom experience, the thesis experience, or the facilities. The teams diagnose the problem and recommend solutions. The thesis committee, for example, devised a more efficient method for matching the students' thesis interests with the appropriate faculty member. The process now flows more smoothly and is less frustrating for the students. Thus the workshop provides an opportunity for people to apply what they've learned to real-life process improvements and benefit by the results.

So Phase 3, Implementation is where we begin to see results from our planning and investment of resources. Also, there are emerging resources to assist in our quality process, such as DVIRC and The Sloan School. Local equivalents of these resources should be accounted for in planning for TQM.

Chapter 9. Phase 4: Diversification

Congratulations, you have arrived! After preparation, planning, assessment, and implementation you are finally ready to move into the fifth and final phase. Here, you capitalize on your experience and success and begin to invite others into the TQM process. Logical candidates for invitation include suppliers and subordinate organizations. TQM not only profoundly changes the manner in which you do business, it also changes how everybody you deal with does business. I've included networking within the scope of Phase 4. Networking capitalizes on the growing number of community, professional, and academic institutions assisting American companies in the quality area, such as DVIRC and the Sloan School I described in the last chapter. The steps necessary to accomplish Phase 4 are included in Exhibit 9-1.

Importance of Supplier Involvement

Suppliers are invited into the quality process for many reasons, but necessity is first and foremost. You can take your own internal quality process just so far before seeking the support of your suppliers. When promising a certain quality of product and service to your customer, with an accompanying delivery schedule, your performance is significantly influenced by your suppliers.

Exhibit 9-1
Phase 4: Diversification

△ **Communication to Suppliers**
  △ Initial Training
    △ Identify Priorities to Select Strategic Suppliers
      △ Modify Competitive Solicitations to Reflect Quality Focus
        △ Supplier Certification
          △ Supplier Reduction Begins
            △ Ongoing Supplier Support
              △ **Communication to Subordinate Organizations**
                △ Initial Coordination
                  △ Initial Training
                    △ Ongoing Subordinate Organization Support
                  △ **Networking**

At Computer One™, rapid growth prompted the pursuit of supplier involvement. In order to continue to grow and meet customer needs, they needed to involve and integrate Apple Computer, Inc., a Fortune 500 company, into their quality process. Suppliers often join in the effort eagerly, because they, too, stand to benefit by such an arrangement. The suppliers gain valuable knowledge about their customers and the end users. This flow of information helps them design more products that better suit their customers' needs.

Computer One™ involves suppliers through monthly meetings, where they discuss product availability and address customer concerns. Working as a team, they strive to get to know the customer better; together, they can answer questions and resolve problems as quickly as possible. Training is another area where the company and its suppliers can join forces. In addition to in-house quality training, Computer One™ associates receive an average of 12 hours of technical training from their various suppliers each month. The company, in turn, provides 4 hour training classes to its large JIT customer, ranging from very basic word processing to advanced desktop publishing.

Some suppliers even provide incentives to companies. For instance, MicroAge has a Peak Performers Program that awards points (which translate into dollar amounts for the winners), based upon annual sales growth for Apple MicroAge dealers. Computer One led the competition in 1991; the company was the number-one top performing Apple MicroAge dealer in the U.S., with a 329% increase over its previous year's purchases from MicroAge. In keeping with the team concept, Computer One distributed the cash award, roughly $1,300 per person, equally among the associates.

Supplier involvement pays off on a broader scale too, enhancing customer satisfaction. One major customer, Sandia National Laboratories, nominated the woman-owned business for a local Small Business Administration (SBA) Administrator's Award for Excellence in 1992. Following an extensive evaluation of business practices—from accounting to technical processes—Computer One won the award. When a customer nominates your company for an award, you can feel confident that you are providing a quality product and following through with exceptional service. And this wouldn't be possible without a smooth, cooperative effort between a company and its suppliers.

Overview of Competitive Process

Before discussing supplier involvement in detail, I will provide a brief overview of the competitive process: how companies (customers) go about contracting for goods and services. This will help clarify where TQM requirements are surfacing in competition for work, and what companies are doing to meet these new challenges.

Whenever a company, or the government for that matter, contracts for goods and services, it packages the requirements in the form of a Request for Proposal (RFP). This document describes specific requirements to would-be suppliers.

Referring to Exhibit 9-2, we see a circular series of events. The cycle begins with your company developing requirements on which suppliers vying for your business would bid. Add to this standard company contractual items, called "boiler plate," such as Drug-Free Workplace, Equal Employment Opportunity, etc., and you have a complete package ready for mailing to potential bidders. Potential suppliers then read this document, prepare their proposal, and submit it to you for evaluation. You award the contract, execute the contract, and eventually close it out.

EXHIBIT 9-2
Contracting for Products and Services

Although a standard process in many organizations, the requirements development segment of the cycle changes significantly as a company implements TQM. Here, Total Quality companies are infusing TQM requirements into the process and gauging suppliers against these requirements in the proposal evaluation stage of the cycle. This is important because it transitions you away from many smaller purchasing actions, which traditionally would have been awarded based upon price alone. These TQM requirements allow you to articulate what has value to you—with price merely being one factor. As a result, your suppliers get fewer, though larger contracts, which assures them of more work from your organization.

For the company practicing TQM, it means spending less time maintaining these contracts. For the suppliers, it means that when they win a contract, they win big. As I described in the earlier examples of Summit Electric Supply and Computer One™, even in difficult times, with diminishing markets and margins, these quality suppliers are gaining an ever-increasing share of the shrinking market. In the case of Summit, this represents an increase of more than 30% per year in sales. For Computer One™, it yielded an increase in annual sales of over 300% last year. So suppliers positioned to respond to these new TQM requirements will win big and prosper even in the most difficult of times. Those who are ill-prepared to communicate their quality process will lose big.

Communication to Suppliers

Clearly, the design and implementation of a TQM process takes time. You need to provide your suppliers a "heads up" on what you are doing in TQM, so they can make intelligent decisions on how to proceed and address this new requirement. You will probably discover that all your existing suppliers will fall into one of three basic categories: (1) They will consider TQM to be a logical extension of their existing management practices. It makes sense, and they will pursue it enthusiastically. In fact today, with so many companies practicing TQM concepts, it is not too unusual for some suppliers to be further along than you are. (2) This group says, "It is unreasonable for our customer to make this request; we just need better customers." These suppliers willingly decide to take their goods and services elsewhere. But as more and more customers begin making similar requests, they may wish they had given the TQM option more consideration. Category (3) encompasses the suppliers who are sitting on the fence. Though attentive when you make your plea, they are not convinced TQM is for them. Some call these companies "the guys from Missouri," the "show me" state. It takes serious effort to convince them of the benefits of TQM.

As quality companies move toward TQM it's not unusual to see a ten-times reduction in supplier count. That means a company with 2000 suppliers of goods and services early in the TQM implementation process could eventually drop to 200. With that drastic reduction, many of the category (3) suppliers go away—not because they were unwilling to change if given sufficient proof of its merit, but because they were too slow to respond. What happened to the category (2) suppliers? They eliminated themselves from the competitive process long ago.

Boeing, the world's number-one commercial aircraft manufacturer, is making a real effort to work more closely with all its suppliers during a time of tremendous change in the way the aerospace industry does business.

Typically, Boeing's outside procurement Quality & Surveillance organization approves two types of companies to provide products and services: direct suppliers, and subcontractors that perform special processes. Boeing wants all suppliers to understand precisely what is expected of them.

Recognizing the need for continuing improvement in supplier quality, Boeing hosted extensive worldwide Supplier Conferences three years ago. A Pareto analysis of the feedback from these meetings identified "COMMUNICATION" as far and away the number-one problem suppliers experienced with Boeing. Since problems are really just opportunities for improvement, Boeing became extremely proactive in tackling this one.

Early in 1991, Boeing released its new "Advanced Quality System for Boeing Suppliers," Document D1-9000. All suppliers who want to be eligible to provide products or services for the Boeing Commercial Airplane Group's new model 777 airliner must be approved to D1-9000. This well thought-out, superbly written document is considered a pace-setting treatise throughout the aerospace industry. In addition to the Basic Quality System requirements already instituted, D1-9000 also requires suppliers to develop Advanced Quality Systems and demonstrate their TQM implementation in initial and periodic audits. This includes top management commitment, team problem solving, training in Statistical Process Control (SPC), and a realistic schedule for full-scale company-wide achievement of TQM.

To ease the transition into this new system of requirements, Boeing works with suppliers before they start the approval process. Boeing holds kickoff seminars in Seattle and around the world, with groups of candidate D1-9000 suppliers. Several junior colleges now teach TQM seminars and classes which focus on meeting the advanced quality requirements of Boeing and many other prime customers. And in addition to auditing these suppliers' ability to meet Boeing's requirements, Boeing Quality and Surveillance Field Operations Managers, well trained and certified in TQM and SPC, help pinpoint areas of confusion and clarify Boeing's philosophy and approval requirements. Further, Boeing provides its suppliers with software for SPC charting, Gage Repeatability & Reliability studies, and Design of Experiments (DOE).

The company has also started inviting larger suppliers into the design stage of new products, the Design/Build concept. Now suppliers have input at the inception of the product—a big improvement from the more familiar practice in our aerospace industry, where products were designed in relative isolation, then thrown "over the fence" from Engineering to Manufacturing. Key players from Boeing Engineering, Manufacturing, and Quality Assurance now work together with prospective suppliers to anticipate problems and develop solutions before production begins.

Initial Training

It is not uncommon to inform your suppliers of your intent to have TQM as a competitive factor during the next round of contract competition or negotiation. Face-to-face training provides suppliers with the basics of what TQM is, shows how it has helped others, and emphasizes how you plan to implement it with those participating in your strategy. This training is roughly equivalent to the Awareness and Orientation training you provide to your employees.

Identify Priorities to Select Strategic Suppliers

You can identify where and how to select strategic suppliers in a variety of ways. In other words, of all the suppliers you have, where do you start to apply quality requirements? I believe one company's story will help illustrate this process.

One location of Siemens, Stromberg-Carlson employs 500 people in the production of telecommunications equipment for GTE and Bell operating companies. A year and a half after beginning a quality process, the company began to approach its suppliers with these concepts. Management knew that in order to achieve higher quality levels and improve cycle times, suppliers must become involved. Establishing tight internal schedules proved useless, for example, if they couldn't get essential components on time.

Initially Siemens brought in suppliers by commodity types, such as electronics components. They explained their quality program and shared the results of customer surveys, emphasizing that their progress depended on the supplier base—especially in terms of cycle times. Under this new approach, called the "Dominant Supplier Program," the Director of Procurement would select one or two major suppliers per commodity code, based upon their commitment to Siemens's improvement efforts. They prioritized the cuts by working a Pareto Principle on the larger dollar and volume items, as well as selecting the most frequently used, essential items.

Before cutting any suppliers, Siemens worked with them individually. For example, if suppliers excelled in terms of delivery performance but had problems with quality levels, Siemens introduced them to TQM concepts and training materials. Training ranged from bringing people into the organization, to actually providing on-site training for smaller suppliers with limited resources. In essence, Siemens customized the supplier training to meet specific needs.

The company also developed a "Ship-to-Stock Program" for suppliers with a good quality record. After careful evaluation on a part-by-part basis, suppliers who have had no rejections for the past year can go on a ship-to-stock basis, without requiring further inspection upon arrival at Siemens. The company and the supplier negotiate a formal agreement, indicating the parts to be treated as ship-to-stock. To achieve this status, the suppliers must have a quality system in place and provide data on their quality levels and reliability testing. In turn, Siemens produces monthly reports, showing how the suppliers rate against their competitors, who are listed anonymously. This information provides incentive for improvement as well as a clear picture of each supplier's strengths and weaknesses. Suppliers also receive quarterly report cards on their delivery and quality performance. Those failing to meet the established goals or objectives are asked to contact the company to discuss possibilities for improvement.

Modify Competitive Solicitations

This is where you express your quality expectations of suppliers in the RFP. I have seen TQM requirements in a variety of industries: health care, distribution, architectural & engineering services, test services, facility maintenance, range support, and manufacturing, to name a few. More and more I am seeing TQM requirements surfacing in competitive solicitations for construction services as well. In construction, as in other industries, the customer is seeking a quality product or service. Offering quality is the admission ticket for consideration for these contracts. Once customers are convinced you offer quality, then they want price. Based upon my experience in bidding for work in the $2 million to $100 million per-year range, this applies to nearly all industries, whether they involve product or services.

An RFP I use in training as "state of the art" in quality requirements for non-manufacturing industries comes from Sandia National Laboratories. This example, for the configuration and delivery of computer equipment, software, and technical support, is indicative of the types of questions I see in other procurements in a variety of industries. The evaluation items, those things being evaluated by the customer in your proposal, are included in Exhibit 9-2.

EXHIBIT 9-2
Example Topics for Evaluation of Supplier Quality System

Evaluation Item	Maximum Points Assigned
10.1 Quality Training	30 Points
10.2 Quality Experience	30 Points
10.3 Quality Policy and Procedures	30 Points
10.4 Management Commitment to Quality	30 Points
10.5 Flow Diagram	55 Points
10.6 Tracking Costs	30 Points
Total Possible Technical Points	**205 Points**

There were three sections being evaluated in the proposal; the cost section where the bidder could earn as many as 300 points, the technical section (700 points), and the administrative section (0 points). Notice that the total possible points a company can receive in its evaluation for quality represents approximately 30 percent of the total technical points awarded (205 of a possible 700 points). This represents a trend in American industries; quality is becoming more important when selecting suppliers. Within the quality section, non-traditional quality assurance/quality control factors come into play, such as Management Commitment to Quality. Here, the customer wants to know how your management communicates a focus on quality; how this message is communicated to your employees, customers, and suppliers; and how you institutionalize the spirit of continuous process improvement.

At one time, a customer might have asked you to explain your quality system with little guidance—something to the effect of, "tell us about your TQM Program." As a result, many of these requirements were poorly done, capitalizing on the sheer imagination of the supplier. I know many of these requirements were prepared poorly....because I helped write some of them. But today, the trend is toward these more specific questions as both customers and suppliers become more astute. The days are truly numbered for suppliers unwilling to take the plunge and implement a quality process. Although I don't recall the author, I remember hearing the following statement, "American companies implementing a quality process may still fail to survive, but any company overlooking the intrinsic benefits of a quality process is a sure loser. To wait may be too late."

Supplier Certification

Quality companies, quality customers, recognize that an up-front investment must be made to move to a strategic supplier base. They also realize this change does not occur overnight. I found Exhibit 9-3 to be insightful. It describes four stages to developing a strategic supplier relationship. At the lowest level (Stage 1) we are constantly at odds with our suppliers; in an atmosphere of basic distrust, things aren't going well. The goal is to arrive at Stage 4, with open communication, a spirit of partnership, and no surprises. Two points must be made here. First, you, as a customer, can have suppliers in different areas, or commodity codes, at varying stages of development. Second, it takes time to transition a supplier through the four stages. Like the rungs on a ladder, each stage is accomplished one step at a time, and if you skip steps you may run the risk of falling. If you have traditionally operated with an autocratic style of management and suddenly walk to the front of the room and tell your people, "we're a team, we're in this together, participative management will become our savior," you can anticipate the blank stares and expressions of disbelief on everyone's faces. You cannot turn around so many years of "tradition" overnight. It's the same for your suppliers, although you probably have greater leverage with your suppliers than with your employees.

EXHIBIT 9-3
The Four Stages of Strategic Supplier Development

Stage 4. A full-blown partnership between customer and supplier, a marriage "made in heaven"

Stage 3. A congruence in mutual goals, a coming together

Stage 2. An arms-length relationship, where adversarial attitudes gradually give way to cautious, tentative assessment of a working relationship

Stage 1. A confrontation with supplier

One company, Quadri Electronics Corporation, accomplished a remarkable turnaround with one particular customer, recovering from behind-schedule deliveries and going on to become a certified supplier for that organization. In this instance, Quadri was manufacturing a major electronic assembly for a government computer. Quadri delivered 60 to 70 assemblies to this customer per month, at about $9,000 apiece. The company earned the contract on the basis of offering the lowest bid, though their quality level met only minimum standards.

Almost from the start of the contract, delivery problems began to surface. Internal quality problems and late deliveries from a major vendor forced Quadri to make late deliveries to this customer, the government. As a result, the customer had to re-procure and buy these parts from Quadri's competition at a much higher price. At this point, Quadri's management made a conscious decision to hold their customer blameless and pay the customer for the re-procurement costs. And even though they were late, they worked to improve customer service. They kept the customer informed on both the problems and the progress. Because of Quadri's cooperation and honest effort to straighten things out, this customer stayed with them.

Quadri personnel not only recovered from past-due deliveries, they also held enough of an internal safety stock to remain on time. Quality has improved to such an extent that the product goes from their shipping dock directly into the customer's stock room—without requiring re-testing or inspection. Within ten months, Quadri went from having severe delivery and quality problems, to becoming the only certified supplier of electronic assemblies this customer has. Additionally, they recently signed a major multi-year contract in a noncompetitive position with this same customer as a result of their performance. The leadership of this company realized that you can only mistreat a customer one time. But by working cooperatively with a customer and meeting your own obligations and responsibilities, even a difficult situation can evolve into a satisfying relationship where everyone is a winner. Creating a turn-around situation as just described requires a tremendous amount of maturity and communication on behalf of both customer and supplier.

Supplier Reduction Begins

Once you've defined what quality is to you through your requirement development process and given your suppliers adequate time to respond to your TQM focus, you begin reducing your supplier count. This typically occurs through the formal bid process you saw in Exhibit 9-2. So what is your reward for making this investment in grooming strategic suppliers?

Siemens in Albuquerque has encountered remarkable results from this effort. Within two years they decreased their total number of suppliers from 800 to 170; circuit board suppliers alone were reduced from 20, down to 3 reliable sources. "You can't form a team with hundreds of suppliers," according to Robert Holkup, their Director of Quality Assurance. But perhaps the most convincing evidence of success can be seen in the improved rejection rates. When their quality process began in the late 1980s, rejection rates averaged between 4-5 percent. Today, rejections are within one-tenth of one percent every month and still improving. Under the old system, Siemens bought commodities based solely on price. If things weren't right, they would chase down replacement parts and remake certain items. This could take a considerable amount of time, and as an end result, the customer suffered a delay in receiving the orders. Now, with fewer rejections, if a problem does arise, Siemens can handle it by working directly with the supplier. Not only is this approach more cost-effective, it eliminates delays and frustration for the customers as well.

Ongoing Supplier Support

After beginning supplier reduction, you provide ongoing support to your strategic suppliers. Typically, this occurs by having more frequent contact with them. With significantly fewer suppliers this task becomes possible, even with constricted resources in the purchasing department. Your largest investment was made early on; now it's reward time. For Computer One this means a regular flow of information to the suppliers, helping them design products which better meet the eventual customers' needs, benefiting both supplier and customer. For Boeing it means implementing ongoing supplier training programs through community colleges and offering supplier seminars. And at Siemens it means providing suppliers with a quarterly report card of their performance. All forms of ongoing support encompass a combination of communication, training, and feedback.

Involving Subordinate Organizations

Subordinate organizations can also benefit from Total Quality Management. When I use this term, "subordinate organizations," I include all business units which are not located in the same proximity to corporate headquarters, or those with different product or service lines. Corporate headquarters can substantially reduce the cost of implementation by serving as a resource for training and internal consulting services to its subordinate business units. Furthermore, your examples may be more relevant to their specific applications—but not always.

I conducted a public workshop on TQM implementation in the summer of 1991. In attendance was a man from Kaiser, a company well recognized in the aluminum manufacturing industry. The Kaiser corporate office sent copies of its training materials to subordinate organizations. This one particular organization had about 60 people specializing in architectural and engineering services. Beyond the basic concepts, we find little application in moving from manufacturing to professional services. Hence, the materials were not well received. So larger organizations with a diversity of subordinate business units should not only offer training, but also translate the examples to each particular niche. It's an investment that pays off.

Communicating your corporate focus on quality is best handled at the executive level, probably during an annual or semi-annual partner or executive coordination meeting. Like Awareness training with your people, it should cover the basics: what TQM is, how others have benefited, etc. Again, it should serve as food for thought. People need time to mull over the concepts. You can probably anticipate the level of receptiveness of these subordinate organization representatives. As such, your time may be well spent building a very strong case for TQM and offering relevant examples.

As I described earlier concerning suppliers, your subordinate organizations will probably fall into three distinct categories. In category 1, they may be very receptive, enthusiastic, and eager to research the subject well beyond the scope of the introductory session you provided. Others occupying this category include business units that simply could not wait for corporate guidance because of customer pressures. Those who fit into Category 2, the ones with their arms folded in gross disbelief when you even suggest they consider doing business differently, should be ignored. There probably isn't anything you can do to motivate these non-believers, until they see pressure from their customers. Those in the middle, "the guys from Missouri" (Category 3), will wait until they see the application of TQM concepts and tools within the company. Many of these people can be swayed to give it a try, if you've demonstrated solid results. For this group, which represents the bulk of your subordinate organizations, you want to be operating on solid footing before expecting them to develop their own quality process.

Initial training at the individual business unit level should follow the same model described in Chapters 5 through 9. That means that before these subordinate organizations begin in-house training, they must make an investment in planning, accounting for their own unique company features: size, culture, product/service mix, etc.

Coordination and ongoing support will typically involve sharing information and training resources in the short term. In the long term, your support will gravitate to sharing experiences, success stories, and serving as a clearing house for company-wide examples of continuous process improvement. Beyond sharing training resources that have been researched and paid for by corporate headquarters, your greatest value is in institutionalizing process improvement among different business units with similar processes, such as payroll, personnel, and purchasing.

Networking

I once helped a client, a professional services firm, bid for work with a "quality company" with rigorous quality requirements. The RFP criteria asked the bidders to describe networking as an integral part of their quality process. Because this isn't an isolated incident, I have included it here as a separate, and important area of Phase 4: Diversification.

Networking means establishing a link to ensure you remain current on issues influencing your industry. It can take the form of active involvement in professional and trade associations. Other sources of information and training can include local trade schools and institutions of higher learning. And today, more community groups are forming to assist local companies in the quality arena.

The Colorado Springs Total Quality Partnership provides support for companies with 50 employees or fewer. This relatively new organization started with an awareness program, holding meetings and giving presentations to small companies as a means of introducing concepts of TQM. Next they began to coordinate resources within the community. They published a newsletter listing related courses and workshops available around the city. They have also started to introduce TQM concepts into local schools, meeting with school representatives and exploring how TQM might apply in the educational area. The Chamber of Commerce and local companies have supported this effort by donating money and services.

Federal government agencies can obtain support from the Federal Quality Institute. The FQI conducts briefings and seminars for senior federal government managers on TQM; assists agencies in the initial steps of TQM implementation; provides advice, information, and documents through its Information Network Services; and administers the President's Award for Quality and the Quality Improvement Prototype Award. It also sponsors an annual conference on federal quality and co-sponsors several regional conferences; publishes handbooks, a quarterly newsletter and special studies on TQM topics; and administers a contract enabling agencies to use a simplified method of obtaining the assistance of private-sector consultants in implementing TQM.

The FQI selects and borrows talented senior federal executives for a two-year period and trains them to conduct its many services. Therefore, the FQI staff has credibility with the federal community, since these executives have managed federal programs and are familiar with the federal environment and its operating constraints. Much of FQI's practical assistance comes from sharing approaches for overcoming common hindrances to improving quality and productivity.

For more information on the services available to federal agencies through the FQI, contact:

> The Federal Quality Institute
> Pension Building
> Box 99
> Washington, D.C. 20044-0099
> (202) 376-3747

Your organization can capitalize on the developing networking opportunities in a number of ways. A company new to TQM, with access to a local group such as the Colorado Springs Total Quality Partnership, has an excellent, inexpensive source of introductory training. To a large company, mature in the quality area, it can be an invaluable resource in helping familiarize suppliers with TQM concepts and tools. In either case, networking is a resource that should be accounted for in any TQM plan.

Chapter 10. Implementation Schedule

In today's world of fast food and instant winners, people often become impatient when forced to wait for something to happen. But some things, like positive change, simply cannot be rushed—especially when it involves people's attitudes and perceptions. One of the best examples of a carefully planned and implemented long-term change process I know of comes from our neighbors to the north in Alberta, Canada.

In 1975, statistical studies on the status of women revealed that although women comprised 45.9 percent of the total workforce of the Alberta Public Service, they represented only 5.7 percent of the management group. Similarly, 1976 statistics showed that women comprised 46.7 percent of the workforce; but 91.5 percent of these women belonged to lowest wage-earning group, as compared to 46 percent of the men. So, in 1977 the Alberta Government established the Personnel Planning and Career Development Unit within the Personnel Administration Office. This unit assumed responsibility for ensuring that all groups of people have the same opportunities for employment and career advancement. The initial priority commitment was "to provide measures to assist female employees in achieving their career potential in the Alberta Public Service."

With the goals and objectives of identifying obstacles to advancement and encouraging practices which help women move ahead, the Women's Program developed through different phases in a planned approach to meeting the original commitment. The first phase, Awareness (1977-1978), was designed to increase the awareness of both males and females of the major obstacles and uncover ways everyone could work together to remove these roadblocks. Phase II, Program Development (1978-1984), focused on developing training programs to assist women in their career advancement. Phase III, Diffusion (1984-1987), concentrated on providing strong support and direction to departments in introducing the initiatives. As the Women's Program moved closer to achieving its ultimate goals, they shifted to Phase IV, Integration (1987-1991). With men and women more fully represented at all levels, many of the special training programs for women were phased out, as they ceased to be needed. Other initiatives were maintained and modified to serve as incentives for assisting all employees in maximizing career opportunities.

This gradual, methodical process has met with very positive results. And because ample time was allowed for these changes to be implemented and accepted, it is highly unlikely that people will revert back to the previous situation. The long-term success of the program speaks for itself. Although participation in the Women's Program has been strictly voluntary, the percentage of women in management in Alberta Public Service has increased from 6.3 percent at the inception in 1977, to 17.9 percent as of December 31, 1991. Positive change with sustainability takes time.

MagneTek, Inc., a manufacturer of electric and electronic products, has 16,000 associates, about 65 locations worldwide, and annual sales of $1.1 billion. In July 1990 they decided to implement TQM. Some relevant milestones are as follows:

❏ **T.E.A.M.* Theme Selected**	**Sep 90**
❏ **Announcement, Search for 3rd-Party Support**	**Oct 90**
❏ **Hired TQM Director**	**Apr 91**
❏ **Formulated Strategy**	**May 91**
❏ **Assessment**	**Jun-Sep 91**
❏ **Pilot at Blytheville, Arkansas**	**Sep 91**
❏ **Executive Committee Review**	**Dec 91**
❏ **Seminar Staff (worldwide) Offsite**	**Jan 91**

* T.E.A.M.: Total Excellence at MagneTek

Cedars-Sinai Medical Center is the third largest non-profit medical center in the country, the largest medical center west of the Rockies. They have 1,200 beds, employ 6,500 people and serve as a major teaching hospital and research institution. Their Quality Initiative (QI) began in mid-1990, focusing attention of the entire organization on customer service; by November 1991 they had concluded interpersonal, analytical, and problem solving training.

An article in *Canadian Manager* describes how to weave positive behavioral changes into a successful quality process. Frances Horibe explains how most companies project a time line for implementing the change to quality from 18 months to 2 years, recognizing that the improvement process is continuous. However, 12 to 18 months into the process, reluctance to change and a basic unwillingness to be honest with oneself surface. We must account for these issues as they become evident. So although we need a solid plan for implementing TQM to set our course and lead us in the right direction, we must realize that the path may need to be altered to account for the dynamics of our people as the change process proceeds.

As we've seen through these examples, implementing TQM takes time. But for those organizations willing to invest the time and allocate the resources, a TQM program can foster dramatic improvements. This chapter describes a realistic schedule for TQM implementation. It also shows the interrelationship between Phases 0 through 4, as discussed in Chapters 5 through 9. Exhibit 10-1 summarizes these interrelationships and provides a detailed schedule.

As you can see in the Exhibit, four specific things must occur for this five-phase implementation approach to work in a coordinated manner. Remember, in Phase 0 resources are committed only to accomplish planning, so the Corporate Council can intelligently decide whether or not to proceed with full implementation.

(1) Initiation of Phase 1, Planning, occurs about mid-way into Phase 0 after making a decision to proceed (step 0.8). This accelerates the decision point whereby the Corporate Council can decide to actually implement the quality process (step 1.13). This planning gives us time to develop the relevant information on which an intelligent business decision can be made.

EXHIBIT 10-1
Example Implementation Schedule

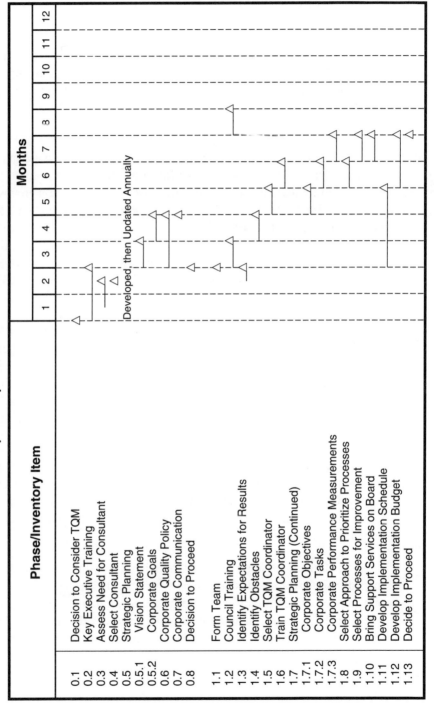

EXHIBIT 10-1

Example Implementation Schedule (Cont.)

Phase/Inventory Item		Months 1–12 (notes)
2.1	Quick-Assessment	
2.2	Self-Assessment	
2.3	Customer Survey	
2.4	Organizational Assessment	
2.5	TQM Planning Inventory	
2.6	Training Feedback	Ongoing from All On & Off-Site Training
3.1	Select Support Personnel	
3.2	Train Support Personnel	
3.3	Management Training	Executives, then Management & Labor
3.4	Workforce Training	
3.5	Form PATs	
3.6	PAT Training	
3.7	Executive Reinforcement	
3.8	First Success Story	
4.1	Communication to Suppliers	
4.1.1	Initial Training	After First Success Story
4.1.2	Identify Priorities to Select Strategic Suppliers	
4.1.3	Modify Competitive Solicitations to Reflect Quality Focus	
4.1.4	Supplier Certification	After First Success Story
4.1.5	Supplier Reduction Begins	After First Success Story
4.1.6	Ongoing Supplier Support	After First Success Story
4.2	Communication to Subordinate Organizations	
4.2.1	Initial Coordination	
4.2.2	Initial Training	
4.2.3	Ongoing Subordinate Organization Support	Ongoing Month 13 and Thereafter
4.3	Networking	Depending on Your Position Within Implementation Process

(2) Once the Corporate Council approves the plan, step 1.13, and decides to proceed, PATs can be formed, and you can begin communicating with your suppliers and subordinate organizations. This is the "heads up" I described in Chapter 9. Although you don't have any results to show them yet, it does plant the seed that something is going on in the TQM area; you've done your homework; and there will be more news as the program progresses.

(3) Support services, step 1.10, must be on-line prior to forming and training the PATs. You want the teams, and the accompanying trainers, consultants, and facilitators, to know the pieces are in place to ensure their success. If team leaders spend too much time rummaging for training materials and don't know precisely where to go for assistance, their enthusiasm will diminish.

(4) Although you've begun communicating to your suppliers and subordinate organizations early on, you cannot expect changes from them until you, yourself, have demonstrated results. So step 3.8 is an important milestone.

I recommended six specific assessment tools in Chapter 7. Now let's consider how and where they are used in the quality process. Exhibit 10-1 shows the quick-assessment as being administered in month 4. Here it's administered to a sampling of all levels within the organization to clarify individuals' expectations for results and anticipate obstacles to our Corporate Council members in the planning process. Certain results surface from this assessment whether you have a small or large sampling for this survey; therefore the ease with which you can administer this assessment should determine exactly how many individuals to survey. An organization with an electronic mail system (a computerized message system) on every employee's desk can clearly solicit and consolidate such information much more easily than an organization that relies on paper with its accompanying lag times.

The self-assessment is suggested as an "icebreaker," something to help bring down barriers and better understand different personality types in forming successful teams. I recommend using it first at the executive level by the Corporate Council, and then at the beginning of the PAT training process.

Both formal and informal customer surveys can be administered at any time. Here I show a formal survey being administered early in month 6. I scheduled it at this point so the Corporate Council would have the benefit of this information in identifying ways to select processes for improvement (step 1.8). Remember, customer input often drives this decision-making process, verifying suggestions from employees and the Council's strategic planning. Most often, as I've said before, no one argues with a focus on certain processes based upon customer input.

I show the TQM Planning Inventory (step 2.5) being administered during the first Council training session (step 1.2). You can include this as part of the Council's training on TQM, "walking them through" the implementation process and building the list of "2-Be-Dones" as they proceed. A good first draft of the implementation schedule can be prepared at the conclusion of this training session transforming the list of "2-Be-Dones" into milestones for implementation. I usually display this with Post-It notes on a series of flip-chart pages taped to the wall.

Finally, training feedback is an ongoing process. It begins with a critique of any off-site workshops Key Executives may have taken in researching for a suitable quality process and continues with any formalized training offered company representatives in any area. Yes, I did say *any* training. As described in Chapter 8, TQM-related training could be very specific and targeted, such as Process Action Team training. Or it could consist of other, already planned for and budgeted training, such as communication skills. In reality, all skills training that improves the work performance of our people constitutes quality training.

The bottom line in Exhibit 10-1 is that a lot of up-front work must be accomplished in order to establish a successful quality process. Unanticipated issues will surface, as they do in any new major corporate initiative, but we do not want to overlook the basics.

So if it takes time to implement TQM, what is the payback? Once your people are trained, the application of these skills to produce results becomes automatic, and subsequent results come more quickly. Marriott Palm Desert, a full-service hotel in Southern California, was built with customer satisfaction in mind. With 895 rooms, five restaurants, two golf courses, and 21 shops and boutiques, the hotel caters to groups and conventions, as well as independent travelers. One day during a weekly staff meeting, the General Manager asked what could be done to improve room service. He said that pre-ordered breakfasts arrived smoothly, within the specified 30-minute time frame, but the call-in breakfast orders took considerably longer to reach the rooms. Under the present system, people who hadn't filled out an order card the night before were penalized by a long wait.

Acknowledging this problem, the hotel management tried a new approach that was planned that very same day and implemented the next. They decided to guarantee everything—the phone will be answered after two rings; accurate room-service orders will be delivered within thirty minutes—or the hotel pays for the meal. Management adopted the plan almost immediately. Not surprisingly, on the first day the hotel bought ten orders. But they tracked the results on a daily basis, recording which meals were bought by the hotel and the reasons why, to find a remedy for the problems. Assessing these results, they realized they needed to add some labor during peak times, cross-train more people, and streamline the kitchen.

By continuously evaluating and improving the processes, great things began to happen within about 90 days. Yes, the hotel did have to buy some meals along the way. But management was so strongly committed to this effort that they printed this guarantee on the menus. As a result of this written guarantee, the guests had higher expectations, so they were more inclined to order meals in their rooms. And meeting planners felt extremely comfortable in selecting this hotel, because they knew the attendees would have no problem with room service. These increases in revenue more than compensated for the meals the hotel had to buy. As an end result, the Marriott Palm Desert went from having consistent problems with room service to leading their region in customer satisfaction. In other words, they went from being the worst to being the very best. This 30-minute guarantee has been so successful that the corporation has now integrated it into nearly all Marriott Hotels.

Chapter 11. Estimating Implementation Resources

This section describes how to "price out" the resources necessary for implementing TQM.

Before top management decides to implement TQM, research is done to help the executives decide whether to commit the time and fiscal resources necessary to undertake an organization-wide change process. The budget line items affecting the cost of TQM implementation include the following:

(1)   Off-Site Training

(2)   Travel and Per Diem

(3)   Time Away from the Job

(4)   TQM Coordinator and Support Personnel

(5)   Training Aids

(6)   Facilities

(7)   Library Materials

(8)   Consulting Support

(9)   Course Development

Off-Site Training, Travel, and Per Diem

Off-site training usually includes attendance at several public workshops, where key executives gather information for the planning and decision-making process. Travel and per diem covers costs such as airfare, food, transportation, and registration fees. As the quality process proceeds, some individuals will attend off-site training periodically to stay abreast of the latest trends in the quality area, to network, and to evaluate new tools for possible use in your organization.

Time Away from the Job

This can constitute the largest cost of implementation, based upon how the organization accounts for employee training time. At worst, it will include all of the employees' time spent in training, attending Process Action Team meetings, and working on PAT-related responsibilities. However, in most instances, time devoted to Awareness and Orientation training can justifiably be included as an overhead item. PAT training and its associated responsibilities should be viewed as part of an employee's routine activities in support of customer projects, depending on the immediacy of the application of their results.

TQM Coordinator and Support Personnel

This expense accounts for the time an individual invests in training, coordinating, consulting, facilitating and other functions which support the quality process. Organizations with hundreds of people can easily justify a full-time person to serve as the TQM Coordinator. Some larger organizations have a cadre of full-time TQM facilitators, although I prefer the approach where part-time support personnel are relied upon. In either case we must account for their time in the budget.

Training Aids

These expenses include reproduction of training materials, binders, overhead transparencies, and assorted office supplies.

Facilities

Facilities expense includes rental fees for the space, meals and refreshments, and audio/visual equipment. These fees routinely apply to the initial training expenses, where training might be held at a remote location to remove the students from the daily flurry of the office. If you use on-site facilities these fees, with the exception of food and refreshments, are usually included in your corporate overhead.

Library Materials

Library materials include the books, original instructional materials, videos and audio-based training, exercises, and texts for researching more sophisticated tools that may apply in the future. This also includes training materials purchased from a vendor, or licensing fees paid to a training/ consulting firm.

Consulting Support

This category covers the initial training and advisory services the organization will need for designing the specific details of its quality process, conducting initial training, and coaching the organization toward success. When working with small companies (100 people or fewer) this can amount to about two days of on-site work per month, plus preparation and close-out time. This estimate can easily become a week or weeks per month for larger organizations, or for clients needing additional help with administering assessments, or conducting extensive internal training before support personnel are in place.

Course Development

Larger organizations typically invest in some form of tailoring for their training packages. This provides the advantage of presenting a consistent image and terminology to effectively communicate the message.

Chapter 12. Concluding Remarks

Observations

I would like to close by commenting on my observations of the American quality movement as an independent third party, someone who regularly witnesses the progress of many organizations in a variety of industries.

First, **everyone is not yet on board**. Although many companies have made great strides in successfully implementing a TQM system, many others are still "sitting on the fence," taking a wait-and-see attitude. Observing these "fence-sitters" reinforces my basic impression that no one undertakes the significant investment of time, effort, and money to pursue TQM without great cause. Although a few visionary leaders do exist, many are waiting to see if sustained pressure will, in fact, surface from their customers.

Second, the **magnitude of self-education** necessary to learn and understand the concepts, principles and tools of TQM is not yet understood...nor appreciated by the American business community at large. I remember taking a class in undergraduate engineering school in dynamics, the study of moving objects, forces, acceleration, and the like. Although I did quite well in what I considered a difficult course, I really didn't understand many of the underlying concepts until several years later, when I began to apply this knowledge to "real-world" problems in industry. TQM is the same way. You must play with the concepts and tools in your own environment, before you clearly recognize how all this fits together.

Third, **quality systems are not transportable**. In September 1991 I was the Chairman for the University of New Mexico's Third Annual TQM Forum. Our luncheon speaker was an entertaining man named Howard Kraye, President of Santa Fe Technologies, Inc., who spoke of his success with self-directed teams. A number of people in the audience scribbled notes fast and furiously, attempting to capture every word. Howard explained the uniqueness of their operation, a start-up company taking great pains to hire people who already have a strong participative/team-player attitude. A start-up company differs from the typical company, generally rich in heritage and cash, though burdened by its accumulated emotional baggage. The point was well-made by Howard. We can all benefit by hearing and learning what has worked and not worked for others, but the ultimate responsibility rests on our shoulders for evaluating and testing these ideas within our own company. Something that works for someone else may not necessarily work for us.

Finally, I see a **variety of motives for companies pursuing TQM**. When visiting a new client, I always ask one important question: "Why are you interested in pursuing TQM?" Although I, personally, am sold on the concept, a surprising number of prospective clients with ample resources are not. If they respond by mentioning emerging customer requirements, a need to catch up to competitors, or the CEO's enthusiasm for the idea, I feel our visit will be mutually beneficial. However, if they say, "Corporate sent us a letter and told us to do so," I know we could be headed for trouble. Those who fall into this latter category generally need the assistance of a specialist to clarify the benefits and applications of the process before seriously investing a lot of resources. From my experience, customers typically have greater leverage in moving an organization toward TQM than any corporate mandate.

What Should You Do Now?

I have four specific recommendations for how you might proceed from here. One is to continue the self-education process. You've actually completed an important milestone in self-education by reading this book. If you are new to TQM, I suggest reading a few more books on the subject to gain a broader perspective and allow your ideas and opinions to gel. The bibliography lists some excellent sources. If you are already well into the quality process, I hope this book sparked some ideas on ways to continue through the process.

Number two is to coordinate with your training department. Regardless of the size of your company, training constitutes a large component of the TQM process. Your TQM Coordinators need to know that they are not alone, that they can capitalize on other assets within the organization. So invest some time in visiting with your training or human resource department, and inform these people of your intentions in this area. They can be a great ally.

Three, realize TQM improves the job you are presently doing. How many times have you left a training session, especially those involving a new management concept, only to ask yourself, "Now what?" The answer to that question generally contains two parts. Part one is the responsibility of the trainer or facilitator. He or she should have imparted enough knowledge and relevant applications of TQM for you to begin applying this information. Part two is your responsibility—to begin applying it. In any in-house training course on TQM, a few individuals always take the initiative to start applying this information short of developing a full-blown implementation plan. These behavioral changes can be subtle. Say, for example, a department receives new guidance on material management. Now, having become familiar with the concept of participative management, the department head would invite the people directly involved in the process to help design the new material management system. Although they are not yet armed with the formal training and problem-solving tools, the basic idea that "two heads are better than one" still applies. So after introductory TQM training, you should take the initiative to apply what you have learned. The basic concepts of working as a team, measurement, and soliciting feedback from customers ("C's" and "c's") are not only important parts of TQM, but also prudent business practices which enable you to do your job better.

And finally, communicate. One underlying theme that surfaces throughout this book is the importance of communication. The healthy exchange of information is not only important to the successful implementation of TQM, but crucial to the preliminary decision-making process. If you, as a CEO or Key Executive, have begun your research into TQM, you'll find logical decision points outlined in this approach. If you choose to proceed, then you must communicate that message so people know what to expect and when. If you decide not to proceed, then you need to communicate that message as well. As I've said before, these decisions are binary—either we proceed, or we don't. In either event, people need to know where they stand.

Quality Trends in America

In the early days of TQM in America corporate leaders thirsted for basic knowledge. What is TQM? Who has succeeded? Today, many organizations have pursued TQM and have seen dramatic results. Some have also seen unsatisfactory results and are ready to move on to yet another fad. So it is important to address this topic in these final pages.

If you are serious about effecting positive change through TQM in your company, it will be helpful to understand how the concept of reengineering comes into play in today's American Quality Movement. On the reverse side of the coin, it is also useful to understand a term emerging in corporate America, Partial Quality Management (PQM). We've all seen companies that practice "Management by Best-Seller," gravitating toward the popular buzz word of the month. Yet as this section shows, all is not lost. There still remains a glimmer of hope in understanding how all these seemingly unrelated, complex concepts mesh together.

We can use our solid background in TQM as a starting point for understanding PQM and reengineering. Partial Quality Management, as the name implies, focuses on one or more selected features of a TQM process. One company might pursue the methodology described in this book—training top management, forming the Corporate Council, selecting processes for improvement, and so forth, whereas another may simply elect to offer customer service training to their front-line counter personnel.

Leadership under the PQM scenario merely approves annual budgets for the Human Resources Department which may not directly correlate to the company's strategic direction. The only teams created in the customer service training would be those formed by the trainer in conducting class exercises. As a result, employees return to the same workplace environment with little discretionary authority to do much more than influence their own behaviors. Because management receives no training on the strategic importance of treating the customers better, there is little support to practice and encourage this array of new-found skills.

In contrast, like TQM reengineering focuses on a process. Teams are formed to understand the process and apply skills for *significantly* improving that process. Reengineering isn't about fixing anything. If TQM is Continuous Process Improvement, achieving small incremental gains in the manner in which we do business, then reengineering is appropriately called Discontinuous Process Improvement (DPI). As with TQM, you begin by understanding the manner in which you presently do business. But the similarities end here. The team begins with a clean sheet of paper to create the process that "should be, " to result in dramatic improvements. To this end, teams are configured and led in a considerably different manner. Under TQM you seek to have many team members with an intimate knowledge of how the existing process operates. However, in reengineering, you intentionally select individuals who have not been tainted by the mindsets of doing things a certain way for the last twenty years. These people will ask the hard questions such as, "Why do we do it that way?"

Because they comprise a large portion of the team, newcomers can leverage their ideas toward "the possible," rather than being tied to "the history" of acceptable performance levels. Reengineering teams frequently serve on a full-time basis. This focus typically causes them to be relocated to a common work area for the duration of the team effort, which can take a year.

Leadership operates differently under reengineering as well. TQM seeks to have the company's top management actively participate, get involved, and show visible support for the Process Action Teams. Conversely, reengineering advocates recognize that the CEO's focus may very well be on processes existing outside the company, as in obtaining venture capital to support a new growth area. In reengineering, top-management commitment is voiced by allowing team members to focus completely on the reengineering team effort.

PQM activities can serve as a stepping stone toward a TQM program. For example "smiles training" can help employees reflect a positive self-image in the eyes of the customer. The next step might involve offering discretionary authority to the front counter people, so they can remedy customer problems independently. Not having to run to a supervisor every time a problem occurs affords speedier service to the customer and creates an impression that the working-level employee has some degree of authority, or empowerment.

Gradually, employees might begin to influence the design of their jobs and the associated processes. Serving as internal customers, they may participate in teams to improve processes that support the front line, such as increasing accuracy in scheduling reservations.

Theoretically, a company could move through a series of events to progress toward a Total Quality operation. However, many companies reach a barrier, finding it difficult to go the next step. This typically occurs when huge investments are required immediately, for a payback far off in the future. Redoing information systems—with the accompanying lead times for computer hardware purchasing, database design, and employee training—represents one such example.

So when does reengineering enter into the picture? Companies turn to it when they discover a dramatic difference in their performance as compared to others, either within or outside their industry. In this case nothing short of revolutionary change will suffice; substantial resources must be committed to close the gap and leap past the competition.

Consider, for example, IBM Credit Corporation, a wholly-owned subsidiary of IBM. If it were an independent company, it would rank among the Fortune 100 service companies. In their early years it took six days on the average, sometimes two weeks, to offer a customer financing on computers, software, and services sold by IBM Corporation. The sales people objected to this lengthy waiting period, as it provided the customer with one to three weeks to take their business elsewhere. IBM Credit tried several fixes, focusing primarily on installing control points and logging procedures. While these "fixes" helped remedy one problem of tracking the status of a credit application in process, they added to the overall cycle time of the process, further compounding the problem.

During a walk-through of the process, two senior managers discovered that the process actually took ninety minutes. The balance of the time was consumed in handling the form within various departments. The problem did not lie in the tasks the employees were performing, rather in the structure of the work processing itself. Reengineering slashed the six-day turnaround to four hours. This single improvement caused sales people to send *one hundred times* more credit applications to IBM Credit. The increase in work load was accommodated without increasing the number of personnel. That's what reengineering is all about— starting with a clean sheet of paper to break down traditional barriers and reinvent traditional business processes.

So how does reengineering fit in the TQM? As it turns out, they dovetail nicely. A senior leadership body, the Corporate Council, must establish priorities for process improvement activities. And since the people who reside on the Council are the same ones who digest competitive information coming into the company to surface major disconnects between their performance and a competitor's, they are the likely candidates to charter and support the reengineering team activities. Thus reengineering and TQM are highly compatible.

Several years ago clients frequently requested a one-hour or a one-day introductory TQM program for their company. Today, however, circumstances have changed dramatically. More astute clients asking tough questions: "How does all of this apply specifically to my company?" "How will this position me to become a vendor of choice to my largest (and most progressive) customers?" "How can I use Quality Management principles to secure more business with existing and anticipated customers?" In today's highly competitive marketplace, few companies pursue TQM simply because it sounds good.

Having witnessed tremendous pressure from competitors and employees alike, many companies are running scared. Therefore, we must reconsider the manner in which we do business. PQM, TQM, and reengineering are not singular options or alternatives. Instead, they lie on a continuum that stretches from PQM at one extreme to reengineering at the other, with TQM residing somewhere in between. When asked which to apply in a particular company, I typically explain that the decision is not yours. Your customers will dictate where you need to operate within this continuum, ranging from PQM to reengineering. But you must decide where to begin. A basic roadmap for change operates somewhat like a weathervane. Innumerable opportunities to effect positive, pro-active change exists within your company, and only you can set the direction and establish priorities. TQM is merely one of many options at your disposal for accomplishing your goals.

Bibliography

Crosby, P.B. Quality Without Tears: The Art of Hassle-Free Management. New York, NY: McGraw-Hill Book Company, 1984.

DiPrimio, A. Quality Assurance in Service Organizations. Radnor, PA: Chilton Book Company, 1987.

Drucker, P.F. Management Tasks, Responsibilities and Practices. New York, NY: Harper & Row, 1974.

Frances, H. "Weaving Habits of the Heart into Quality Management." Canadian Manager. Vol. 16, Issue 3, Sept. 1991, pp. 21-24.

Girard, J. with S.H. Brown. How to Sell Anything to Anybody. New York, NY: Warner Books, 1979.

Hammer, M. and J. Champy Reengineering the Corporation: A Manifesto for Business Revolution. New York, NY: Harper Collins Publishers, 1993

Hansen, Richard L., Capt., USAF. An Overview to the Application of Total Quality Management. Aeronautical Systems Division ASD/CCT, Wright-Patterson AFB, OH.

Hull, K. and D. Neptune "A New Tool for Creativity: Improved Decision Making." The Journal for Quality and Participation. Vol. 14, No. 5, September 1991.

Iacocca, L. with W. Novak. Iacocca: An Autobiography. New York, NY: Bantam Books, Inc., 1984.

Jensen, R. "Total Quality Control: Does Japan Have a Competitive Edge?" Border-Trax (USA/Mexico Version). April 1991, p. 18.

Lamprecht, J., Ph.D. "The ISO 9000 Certification Process: Some Important Issues to Consider." Quality Digest. August 1991, pp. 61-70.

Management Practices: U.S. Companies Improve Peformance Through Quality Efforts. United States General Accounting Office Report to the Honorable Donald Ritter, House of Representatives. GAO Report Number: GAO/NSIAD-91-190, May 1991.

Miller, J.C. III (Signatory). Quality Improvement Prototype, Internal Revenue Service-Federal Tax Deposit System - Department of the Treasury. Office of Management and Budget.

National Institute of Standards and Technology. "1990 Application Guidelines: Malcolm Baldrige National Quality Award."

Pfeiffer, J.W. Ph.D., et al. Shaping Strategic Planning: Frogs, Dragons, Bees, and Turkey Tails. San Diego, CA: Scott Foreman Professional Books in association with University Associates, Inc., 1989.

Process Quality Management and Improvement (PQMI) Guidelines. Issue 1-1, by AT&T Quality Steering Committee, Published by AT&T Bell Laboratories, 1987.

Quality Progress. (Glossary of Terms) Milwaukee, WI: American Society for Quality and Participation, Feb. 1992.

Sandia National Laboratories Request for Quotation for Systems Ordering Agreement, Document Number 66-4904, June 29, 1990.

Savage, E. W. "Total Quality Is Total Change." Journal for Quality and Participation. Vol 14, Issue 5, Sept. 1991, pp. 100-107.

Schonberger, R.J. World Class Manufacturing: The Lessons of Simplicity Applied. New York, NY: The Free Press, 1986.

Spanbauer, S. J., Ph.D. <u>A Quality System for Education</u>. Milwaukee, WI: ASQC Quality Press, 1992.

Steinburg, C. "Taking Charge of Change." <u>Training & Development</u>. American Society for Training and Development, March 1992, pp. 26-32.

Walton, M., with Foreword by W.E. Deming. <u>The Deming Management Method.</u> New York, NY: Dodd, Mead & Company,

Walton, S. with Huey, J. <u>Sam Walton: Made in America, My Story</u>. New York, NY: Doubleday, 1992.

Glossary

Benchmarking -An improvement process in which a company measures its performance against that of best-in-class companies, determines how those companies achieved their performance levels, and uses the information to improve its own performance. Benchmarking can compare strategies, operations, processes, and procedures.

Brainstorming - A technique for generating numerous ideas using the composite talent and experience of a group in a facilitated meeting environment.

Cause-&-Effect Diagram - A graphic technique for summarizing the results of a brainstorming session, identifying the causes of a specified undesirable outcome. Also referred to as "Fishbone Diagrams" and "Ishikawa Diagrams" (after the developer, Professor Kaoru Ishikawa of Tokyo University).

Control Chart - A graphic technique for identifying whether an operation or process is in or out of control and tracking the performance of that operation or process against calculated control and warning limits.

Corporate Council - The corporate entity responsible for chartering Process Action Teams, committing corporate resources, removing barriers to process improvement, and participating actively in the TQM initiative. The Corporate Council includes the organization's Chief Executive Officer/President and top representatives from each of the organization's functional areas (i.e. Marketing, Operations, Administration, etc.).

Crosby, Philip - The founder and chairman of the board of Career IV, an executive management consulting firm. He also founded Philip Crosby Associates, Inc. and the Quality College. Author of *Quality is Free*, *Quality Without Tears*, *Let's Talk Quality*, and *Leading: The Art of Becoming an Executive*. Crosby, who originated the zero defects concept, is an ASQC senior member and past president.

Deming Prize - Award given annually to organizations that, according to the award guidelines, have successfully applied companywide quality control, based on statistical quality control. Although the award is named in honor of W. Edwards Deming, its criteria are not specifically related to Deming's teachings. There are three separate divisions for the award: the Deming Application Prize, the Deming Prize for Individuals, and the Deming Prize for Overseas Companies. The award process is overseen by the Deming Prize Committee of the Union of Japanese Scientists and Engineers in Tokyo.

Deming, W. Edwards - A prominent consultant, teacher, and author on the subject of quality. After sharing his expertise in statistical quality control to help the U.S. war effort during World War II, the War Department sent Deming to Japan in 1946 to help that nation recover from its wartime losses. Deming has published more than 200 works, including the well-known books *Quality, Productivity and Competitive Position* and *Out of the Crisis*. Deming, who developed the 14 points for managing, is an ASQC Honorary member.

Design of Experiments - A branch of applied statistics dealing with planning, conducting, analyzing, and interpreting controlled tests to evaluate the factors that control the value of a parameter or group of parameters.

Executive - A member of the top two levels of the organizational chart. Those individuals responsible for the strategic course of the organization, generally consisting of the CEO/President, deputies, and functional managers who may be Vice-Presidents, Directors, etc.

80-20 - A term referring to the Pareto principle, first defined by J.M. Juran in 1950. The principle suggests that most effects come from relatively few causes; that is, 80% of the effects come from 20% of the possible causes.

Facilitator - An individual with excellent communication and interpersonal skills who conducts organized meetings and encourages the group to arrive at a consensus on issues involving the members of the group.

Flow Chart - A graphic technique using symbols to identify the operations involved in a process, their interrelationships, inputs, and outputs. A basic tool of TQM, flow charting routinely comprises the first step in understanding selected processes in an organization.

Juran, Joseph M. - The chairman emeritus of the Juran Institute and an ASQC Honorary member. Since 1924, Juran has pursued a varied career in management as an engineer, executive, government administrator, university professor, labor arbitrator, corporate director, and consultant. Specializing in managing for quality, he has written hundreds of papers and 12 books, including *Juran's Quality Control Handbook, Quality Planning and Analysis* (with F.M. Gyrna), and *Juran on Leadership for Quality.*

Just-in-Time (JIT) - A system of doing business where processes are understood well enough to produce and deliver paper, information, and/or product to a customer just prior to their use by the customer.

Key Executives - A small portion of all corporate executives who are routinely consulted first on important issues confronting the organization.

Management - Individuals who supervise the workforce directly or indirectly and/or manage individual projects; responsible for accomplishing short-term organization objectives.

Management Commitment - A commitment of corporate resources, including executive and employee time, to the Total Quality improvement process.

Pareto Chart - A tool for ranking causes from most significant to least significant. It is based on the Pareto principle, first defined by J.M. Juran in 1950. The principle, named after 19th-century economist Vilfredo Pareto, suggests that most effects come from relatively few causes; that is, 80% of the effects come from 20% of the possible causes. The Pareto chart is one of the basic tools of quality.

Pareto Diagram - A graphic technique that uses data to help PAT members identify where scarce resources should be applied to reap the greatest gains. It helps to prioritize options, portraying the results as a bar diagram.

Partial Quality Management (PQM) - A company strategy employed to address one or more features of a Total Quality Management Process such as leadership, information systems, customer satisfaction, human resource development, etc.

Process - A series of operations or activities linked together to provide a result that has increased value.

Process Action Team (PAT) - A group of four to eight members that applies the principles and tools of TQM to (1) identify opportunities for process improvement, (2) understand existing processes and identify where the greatest gains can be realized from process improvement, (3) provide recommendations for process improvement, and (4) implement process improvement.

Quality - The attributes of a product or service that the customer values. Depending on the customer's focus, "Quality" may include surface finish, timeliness, size, cost, reliability, or other factors.

Reengineering - A strategy for process improvement that employs dedicated teams to understand and significantly improve the manner in which they do business.

Taguchi Methods - The American Supplier Institute's trademarked term for the quality engineering methodology developed by Genichi Taguchi. In this engineering approach to quality control, Taguchi calls for off-line quality control, on-line quality control, and a system of experimental design to improve quality and reduce costs.

Total Quality Management (TQM) - A cooperative form of doing business that relies on the talents and capabilities of both labor and management to continually improve quality and productivity using teams.

TQM Coordinator - The individual charged with the overall responsibility of ensuring that the "mechanics" of implementing TQM are carried out. He/she serves as a trainer, facilitator, coordinator, and organizer of TQM-related resources and maintains statistics on the progress of Total Quality.

Geographically close to the CEO/President on the corporate organizational chart, the TQM Coordinator is consulted on issues related to the corporate quality initiative and serves as the Secretary to the CEO/President during Corporate Council meetings.

Variation - A change in data, a characteristic, or a function that is caused by one of four factors: special causes, common causes, tampering, or structural variation.

Workforce - Those individuals responsible for accomplishing the day-to-day activities of the organization, interacting with customers, and creating the impressions necessary to form and cement positive customer attitudes toward the company.

Zero Defects - A performance standard developed by Philip B. Crosby to address a dual attitude in the workplace: people are willing to accept imperfection in some areas, while, in other areas, they expect zero defects. This dual attitude has developed because of the conditioning that people are human, and humans make mistakes. However, the zero-defects methodology states that, if people commit themselves to watching details and avoiding errors, they move closer to eliminating all defects. The optimal performance standard is "zero defects," not "close enough."

Index

TECHNICAL MANAGEMENT
CONSORTIUM, Inc.

The Company

Consulting Services: This Division specializes in the design and implementation of Total Quality Management (TQM) systems for private and public-sector organizations. TMC representatives also facilitate team meetings and training sessions. Responding to America's emerging need for bringing suppliers into the quality process, TMC helps develop quality requirements for competitive solicitations and assists companies, both large and small, in writing proposals that address these new requirements.

Training Services: This Division offers a variety of training programs on TQM:

> Implementing Total Quality Management -- 1 to 3-Day Program
> TQM in Government Contracting -- 1 to 2-Day Program
> The "Tools of TQM" -- 1/2 to 3-Day Program
> Facilitator/Train-the-Trainer -- 4 to 8-Day Program
> Introduction to TQM -- 1-Hour to 1-Day Program

Speaker Services: Keynote and breakout presentations for conferences, conventions, and executive off-site forums.

Products Division: This Division specializes in the design, development, marketing, and order fulfillment of products related to TQM. Products include books, audio and videotapes, and computer software. Clients may select from a variety of off-the-shelf products, or contract for customized products designed to serve their specific purposes.

Training programs may be tailored to meet your organization's needs.
Please call for details. (505) 299-3983

Order Form

Three Ways to Order
1. Call:
    (505) 299-3983
2. FAX to:
    (505) 299-5788
3. Mail to:
    Technical Management Consortium, Inc.
    P.O. Box 13591
    Albuquerque, New Mexico 87192-3591

Name: _____

Title: _____

Company: _____

Address: _____

City: _____ State _____ Zip _____

Telephone: (____) _____

( )_____ **Book:** Revised 2nd Edition, *Implementing TQM: Competing in the Nineties Through Total Quality Management*
ISBN 1-878821-09-1 $17.95 each, soft cover

( )_____ **Workbook:** *Implementing TQM: Competing in the Nineties Through Total Quality Management,* A companion product for the book and Audio Cassette.
ISBN 1-878821-06-7, $25.00 each

( )_____ **Audio Cassette:** 2nd Edition, *Implementing TQM: Competing in the Nineties Through Total Quality Management*
(90 minutes, 45 each side) ISBN 1-878821-04-0 $19.95 each

( )_____ **Book:** *Prosper Through Leadership: Succeeding In Tough Times,*
ISBN 1-878821-08-3, $19.95 each, hard cover

Quantity Discounts Available
Add $5.00 Postage & Handling for Each Order
New Mexico Residents Add 5.82% Gross Receipts Tax

Method of Payment
    ( ) Full Payment Enclosed - Make check or P.O. payable to:
    Technical Management Consortium, Inc.
    ( ) MasterCard
    ( ) Visa

        Card Number: _____

        Expiration Date: _____

        Signature: _____

For more information on *Speaking, Training* and *Consulting Services*,

Call **(505) 299-3983**